D1692369

STARTUP EUROPE

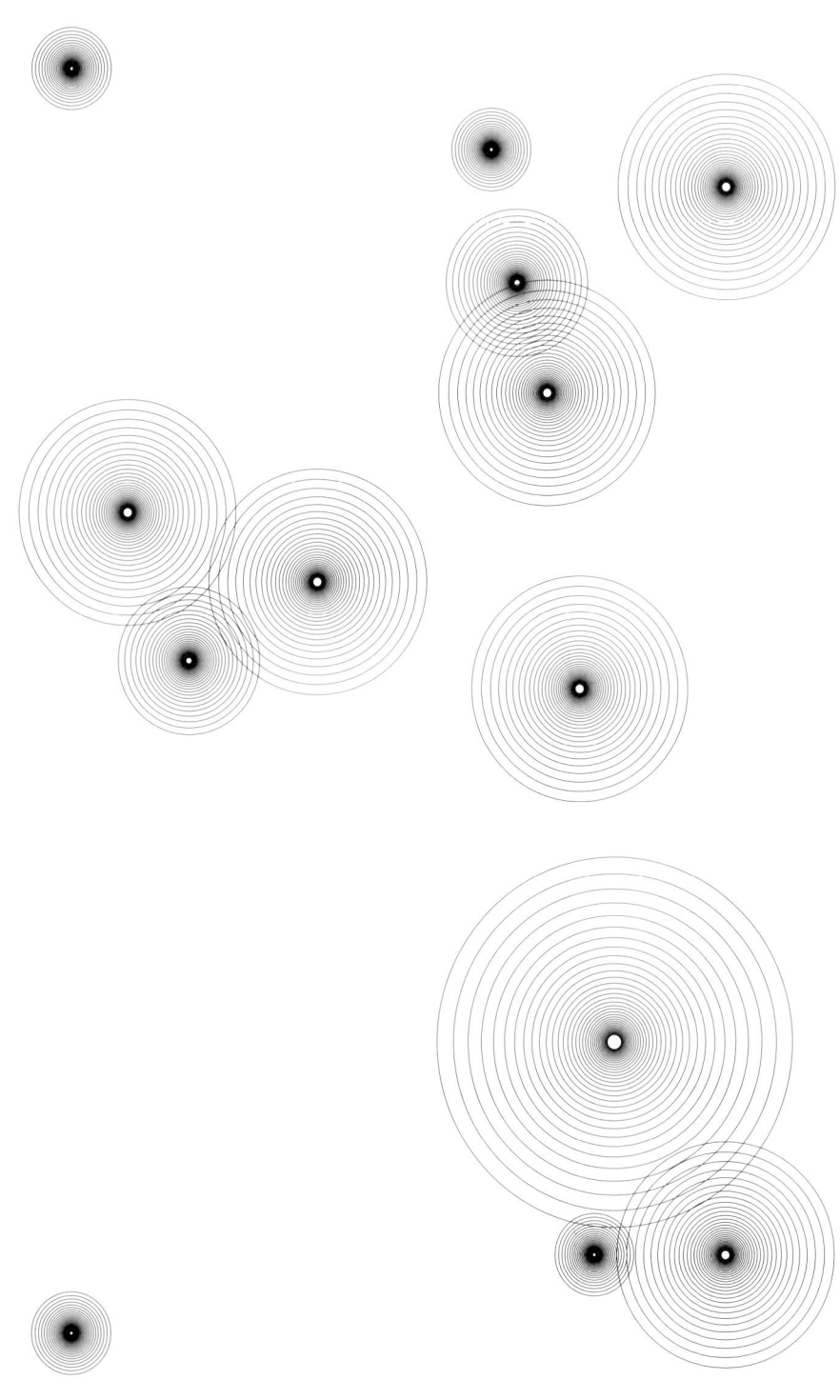

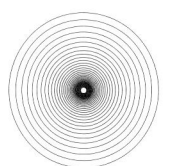

STARTUP EUROPE

The entrepeneurs transforming Europe

Skaperkraft
THINK TANK

FF
FREKK FORLAG

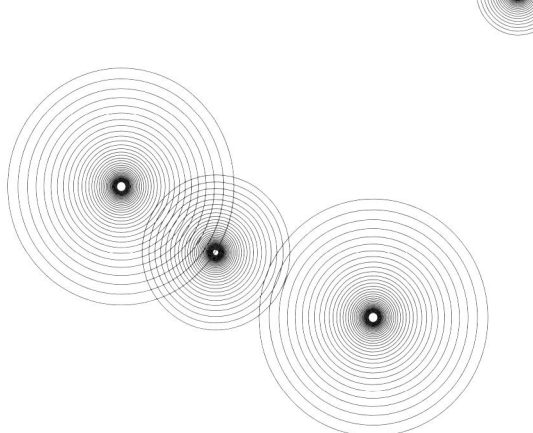

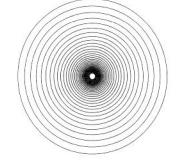

P. 8 *Preface*

P. 12 INTRODUCTION

P. 19 Part 1 ENTREPRENEURSHIP WORKS:

Chapter 1: THE ENTREPRENEURIAL SCENE / BERLIN
LGBTs, artists, and students have created a culture that many entrepreneurs find attractive. And with property prices among the lowest in Europe, it's a boomtown for Europe's new creative class.

Entrepreneur 1: THE ENTREPRENEURIAL ADDICT / BERLIN
When Russian-born Gleb Tritus realized he could make money by optimizing text content on search engines online, he was hooked. The young serial-entrepreneur is now addicted to one thing: starting new ventures.

Chapter 2: THE ENTREPRENEURIAL STATE / ESTONIA
The Estonian government may have understood before anyone else that technology could make their country wealthy. After "Skype" and "Transfer Wise" became breakthrough hits, it became obvious to everyone.

P. 63 Part 2: FROM CONCEPT TO INDUSTRY?

Chapter 3: THE SEEDS OF SUCCESS / LISBON
The entrepreneurs of Lisbon had a dream: that their city would become the California of Europe.

Entrepreneur 2: THE PERSISTENT LOGISTICS EXPERT
From a functional and modest Lisbon office, mathematician Filipe Carvalho is growing one of Portugal's most successful IT startups through software that slashes both cost and pollution.

Chapter 4: THE PROTOTYPE FACTORY / OSLO
In Oslo more and more workshops are popping-up where one can produce less expensive prototypes.

Entrepreneur 3: THE LIVING AVATAR
In less than a year Karen Dolva has gone from idea to market with her Avatar-robot. While the robot will move chronically sick children back to their classrooms, she moves the seed money that makes scaled production possible.

P. 123 Part 3: WORK FOR ALL

Chapter 5: THE MIRACLE OF JOBS
Through its tax and welfare policy the UK government is encouraging Britons to start businesses. Now, both unskilled workers and labour migrants are finding work at startups.

Entrepreneur 4: THE STUBBORN BIKER
Failure is just something to learn from thinks Birmingham-based biker-turned-manufacturing entrepreneur John Miller. From a slow start in 1999, his company now makes composites for Formula 1 racing cars and spacecraft.

P. 162 Part 4: APPENDIXES

Money makes the world go round
Research to the people – that´s the thing
The entrepreneur who built Norway

We travelled to European cities and studied their startup ecosystems. We wanted to tell a story about success, but also about learning from mistakes.

8

STARTUP EUROPE

9

12

STARTUP EUROPE

Almost a third of all young adults in the EU live at home. Europe needs entrepreneurs that create products that consumers want and thereby lift their friends out of unemployment.

In Tallinn young people from all over the world take part in a technological boom that has made Estonia the European country with the highest number of entrepreneurs per capita.

According to French economists at CEPII (Centre d'Etudes Prospective et d'Informations Internationales) Estonia will reach the level of the Nordic countries, measured by GDP per capita, in only ten years.

This boom has given the small Baltic country growing self-confidence after the fall of the Soviet Union. It is also an example of a growing gap between richer and poorer countries on the continent.

EMIGRATE OR LIVE WITH YOUR MUM

It is different elsewhere - in Spain, Italy, Slovenia, Portugal and even Sweden, many young people are struggling to get their adult-life going. In the EU every third male and every fourth female between the age of 25 and 29 live at home. The problem is worse in southern Europe.

Without work and living with mum well into their 20s makes it hard for many to create families of their own. It also destroys self-confidence.

With youth unemployment rates rocketing to between 20 and 50 per cent in several countries, the future looks grim. To realize their dreams many emigrate. In 2014 a million south and east Europeans moved to Germany. Almost two per cent of Portugal's population has emigrated since 2010.

The political system is often a barrier. In Serbia we did not meet a single entrepreneur who didn't mention corruption as a major problem. In Lisbon we continuously heard about an overwhelming bureaucracy and a political elite who cover-up the deficits of established, state-owned companies.

When citizens do not trust the state to manage public resources well, incentives to start new businesses vanish. Simultaneously, queues at social security offices grow.

WHERE JOBS ARE CREATED

However, in Berlin, angel investors look for good ideas and promising business talent. Youth unemployment in Germany is at a record-low 4.9 per cent. Fewer young people live at home now than in 2007. Here, the paradox is that fewer people start new businesses, but there is strong growth at technology-based startups and of female entrepreneurs.

The Minister of Commerce, Sigmar Gabriel, has a vision for Germany: Entrepreneurship is now defined as "a third career-path". Since 2007 millions of Euros has been channelled to build incubators at universities combined with more scholarships for incumbent entrepreneurs.

Gabriel's vision clearly indicates the direction Europe needs to follow. It is only when young people venture into the unknown in greater numbers, hire their peers, and create the services and goods consumers demand that new growth will come.

That's exactly what's happening in the United Kingdom. The country is experiencing a wave of entrepreneurship in almost all industries. Since 2011 unemployment has fallen from 8.5 to 5.1 per cent. As professor Mark Hart points out later in the book, the Brits are among the most entrepreneurial in Europe.

Entrepreneurs have created 40 per cent of the new jobs. The government has followed suit, unleashing tax-reforms giving incentives to invest in small and medium-sized businesses. Today, a swarm of business-angels hovers over the country.

Despite these success stories few European companies grow to be world-leading. Evidence of this is the fact that none of the world's largest IT companies are European.

DON'T TRY THIS ON YOUR OWN

The reasons for northern Europe's struggle are manifold. Many countries such as Norway, the UK and

Germany face challenges in their school systems. Too few with good technical skills are educated, thus startups struggle to find competent employees. Schools also do not teach students to take risks.

In the south a major problem is that economies do not grow fast enough. Since 2010 all continents, except Europe, have experienced growth. Neither Greece, Portugal nor Italy has shown the competitive edge to succeed.

In Startup Europe we try to stimulate students, entrepreneurs and politicians to heighten their ambitions. For – should there be any doubt – weak competitive abilities and stagnant youth unemployment are the basis of a tragedy. And it will be tragic if Europe's young get used to the idea that everything was better in the past.

Introduction

Part 1
ENTREPRENEURSHIP WORKS:

Berlin and Tallinn have over the past 25 years transformed themselves from planned economies to dynamic societies. Entrepreneurs were crucial for their success.

Berlin
THE ENTREPRENEURIAL SCENE

LGBTs, artists, and students have created a culture that many entrepreneurs find attractive. And with property prices among the lowest in Europe, it's a boomtown for Europe's new creative class.

So there I was, in the basement of a club in Karl Marx Allé, Berlin. Getting in hadn't been easy. Coming down the stairs, I'd had to weave through an uncommonly long procession of offers for free take-away from a dozen local restaurants. The establishment's clientele were obviously frequent consumers of take-away food.

I received a name badge, some drink coupons, and a beer. The music got ever louder as the evening progressed. All around me, several hundred people, mainly in their 30s, mingled. It was a party. A *"gründerfest"*. In 2014, entrepreneurs (*gründers*) made up 2.8% of Berlin's population. That makes Berlin the most enterprising city in the country, followed by Hamburg and Munich.

Everyone was here for the same reasons, we were mingling and networking. To simplify things, we'd been issued different coloured cords. Yellow was reserved for entrepreneurs, investors had been given white, and red ones had been given to service providers. Yellow cords were the most numerous, white the least. But even without the coloured cords, it was easy to see who was who. The yellows were dressed more edgily, the whites more conservatively. Red cords often dangled in front of a uniform of some sort.

As I looked around and saw all the drinks being picked up at the bar, it struck me: It would be impossible to get any closer to the cliché image of Berlin as the city where entrepreneurs party all night long while building-up their business. In Germany entrepreneurship has become cool – particularly for men (most entrepreneurs are still male) preoccupied with the preferences of German women. An AXA study from January 2015 showed that nearly half of all German women found entrepreneurs more attractive than regular employees. Only 13 per cent of women surveyed respected permanent employees more than entrepreneurs.

Positive perceptions notwithstanding, most of the people wandering alone around the room were wearing yellow cords. Reds stood in groups. Crowds had formed around white cords. It was time to start mingling and find someone to talk with. A man in a dark suit, red tie, and red cord saw my yellow entrepreneur's cord.

"I can help make your business ideas a reality." Willebrand from the Berliner Sparkasse was making a sale.

When he found out that I wasn't a real gründer, but writing a book on entrepreneurship, he was a little disappointed. But it seemed he thought that all publicity is good publicity, because he continued to explain enthusiastically. Willebrand worked for the bank's *Firmen Center für Gründung und Nacthfolge* (Business Centre for Establishment and Following Up).

"This branch's main responsibility is aiding entrepreneurs. We help them set up a business plan, a liquidity budget, and we also have specialized loans for entrepreneurs. In addition, we offer free consultations on how to set up the financial aspects of the business."

AN ADVANCE WARNING OF THE EUROPEAN CRISIS

The growth of the entrepreneurial scene has been a huge boom for Berlin. For a long period, the city was on the brink of bankruptcy. Until the division of Germany into the eastern Deutsche Demokratische Republik (DDR) and the western Bundesrepublik Deutschland (BRD), Berlin and the Ruhr region were the twin industrial powerhouses of Germany. But capitalist companies feared having their assets seized, and in 1945 key Berlin companies such as Siemens, Deutsche Bank, and AEG moved as far away from East Germany as they could, to the West German cities of Munich and Düsseldorf. Few new industrial businesses were established in West Berlin during the cold-war era.

After the fall of the Berlin Wall, much of the heavily subsidized, state-owned East German industry went out of business, having lost much of its competitive edge over the preceding 40 years. As a result, the number of jobs for unskilled workers fell drastically in the 90s, with a corresponding rise in unemployment. This bears obvious similarities to present-day Europe. The current situation, particularly in Southern Europe, is a carbon copy of the situation in Berlin during the 90s. Southern Europe is not supplying enough of what the world is demanding. But all of Europe will have to change in the coming years.

The world is in the midst of the 4th industrial revolution (see part 2). During the next couple of years digitalisation and automatization will change the way we work and live. If Europe does not manage the transition to a digital economy, unemployment and low growth will persist. Although there is an entrepreneurial boom in Berlin, the industrial core is still small. Unemployment is the second highest in Germany, five per cent higher than the national average, and over three times as high as in Bavaria. Berlin's Gross Domestic Product (GDP) per capita is 90 per cent of the German average, and only 60 per cent of Hamburg's. In this respect, the current entrepreneurial boom is just what the city's business sector needed. Entrepreneurs are customers with unconventional needs. They eat take-away in the middle of the night and change offices every time the company expands. Several banks have specialized account managers and offers to reach entrepreneurs, who often lack liquidity, but not expenses.

Gradually, a number of businesses that help entrepreneurs survive and prosper have evolved. One such business is the real estate agent Colliers. Marcus Lehmann is head of the company's rental division. He explains why newly established businesses move around a lot.

"Office space is a big problem for entrepreneurs in Berlin. It's not that there isn't enough space, but as the buildings in the reasonably priced areas of the city centre are old, rooms are often either too big or too small."

Office-spaces may be well suited to a startup with five employees, but what to do when you grow to ten? If a business really takes off, the company may have to scale up to 50 employees within the space of a few years.

"I know a lot of companies that have offices in five or six locations around the city. It makes having meetings complicated, and a lot of time is spent travelling between offices. That's the sort of thing we help our clients avoid."

While some people try to sell services to growing enterprises, others want a potential slice of any new cake. These are "angel investors". An angel investor doesn't need to see immediate returns, and is willing to take more risk than other investors. Bernd Grosse Lordemann is an angel investor working for the film company DCM.

"We do film production, rentals, and angel investment. That is to say, we work on the creative, entrepreneurial side of the movie business. The owners of DCM have all sprung from the Berlin entrepreneurial scene, and they want to continue to be part of it."

I was left wondering, do other European entrepreneurs with good ideas come to Berlin to participate in this sort of thing? This proved to be the case; Austrians, Serbs and Portuguese are here. Berlin is becoming a melting pot of entrepreneurial luck-seekers. No wonder, I was struck by how simple it was to get in touch with both investors and entrepreneurs.

FEWER ENTREPRENEURS

Dr Marc Evers' surroundings are completely different from a cellar club in East Berlin. He works on the fifth floor of a new building behind Berlin's *Stadtschloss* (city palace), which is being built on the land of the old East German government headquarters. Here, you'll find the *Deutscher Industrie und Handelskammertag* (DIHK: the Association of German Chambers of Industry and Commerce). Their main office is one of many in Berlin built after the capital was moved from Bonn in 1999. Evers works with entrepreneurship and innovation. Every year he makes a survey of entrepreneurship in Germany, and in 2014 he made a number of exciting discoveries.

First, the number of entrepreneurs in Germany had fallen. This is due to the fact that necessity driven entrepreneurs are decreasing in number.

Entrepreneurs of this nature start their own business because they can't find suitable employment. When the job market is good, as it is in Germany now, this type of person prefers permanent employment to starting his or her own business.

Second, the number of opportunity-driven entrepreneurs had risen. These are people who start a business because they *want* to be entrepreneurs. Not to mention that since 2006 the number of IT-entrepreneurs had doubled. As women began thinking more highly of entrepreneurship, the number of female entrepreneurs rose significantly.

On the surface, these seem like positive developments. Fewer people are starting businesses because they have to, while more people are dreaming of realizing their own ideas. Berlin is a driving force at the centre of this development. According to DIKH-Berlin, entrepreneurs in Berlin created 33,800 new jobs in 2014 alone.

CHEAP LEASES IN TRENDY NEIGHBOURHOODS

There are several reasons for these developments, but some facts are more relevant. Rent is cheap in Berlin. Admittedly, it is rising at record speed, but it is still lower than similar metropolises elsewhere in Europe or in the US. In addition, Berlin has excellent research and education infrastructure, including three universities and a number of research institutes.

This meant that in August 2015, an entrepreneur in Berlin could pay 1,000 euros a month for an apartment that would cost twice that amount in Oslo, London, or Paris. An entrepreneur making €1,500 net in Berlin has the same standard of living as a person making €2,500 in Oslo or €2,800 in London. Low rent is an important factor in making Berlin attractive to people with dreams. Berlin has become a city of immigrants. In 2012, there were almost 500,000 foreign nationals living in Berlin. Many of them are entrepreneurs. In fact, one in five entrepreneurs in Germany is an immigrant.

However, history is just as important. When the Wall divided the city, West Germans could avoid military service by moving to Berlin. That meant that the city attracted a fairly extensive alternative scene, including artists, LGBTs, and political non-conformists, who wanted to escape the conservative West. Over time, the finances of both students and LGBTs improved. Artists remained poor, but they started to attract people who wanted to live in a vibrant neighbourhood, and gentrification took off.

A 24/7 culture evolved. As a result, Berlin restaurants and bars close at 4 or 5 AM, unlike at 2 AM as they do in Munich. Entrepreneurs working till late at night can still grab a beer or a bite after work. Several Berlin companies cater to this flexibility; one of them is Foodora, a home-delivery service used by fancy restaurants.

A tolerant culture and cheap offices made starting business incubators and eventually coworking places easy. This led to a culture that many entrepreneurs enjoy.

THE GRASS ROOTS MOVEMENT IN KREUZBERG

"For us, it all started in 2008. We were six self-employed people: a lawyer, a political consultant, a product designer, all of us looking for professional office space," says CEO and co-founder of Betahaus, Max von der Ahé.

They were tired of sitting in cafés, but didn't want to sit in regular offices either.

"A coworking space bridged that gap, but at the time, there weren't a lot of places like this in Berlin."

He pauses.

"I have to underscore the fact that this whole city was different in 2008/2009. At the time, the grass roots movement and the DIY-attitude (do it yourself) were booming. This place had been an old printing shop and sponge factory, but was only rented out 50 percent at the time. In fact, there were still a lot of free spaces in Kreuzberg."

This empty space made it possible for businesses to grow from the bottom up. Individuals tried their luck in the city and started companies, galleries, and cafés. Betahaus as an institution serves as the embodiment of the area's transformation. At the end of the 70s, Kreuzberg was an isolated and impoverished district in West Berlin. It was the heart the punk scene, and a melting pot with over 160,000 Turkish inhabitants. Today, Kreuzberg boasts one of the youngest populations in Europe, and is the source of much of Berlin's entrepreneurial and alternative culture.

"We started developing the building. First, we filled up one room. Then, we opened a new door and filled up another room. Since the whole place was empty, we were able to expand without investors and virtually for free."

Currently, there are more than 50 coworking offices in Berlin. A large number of them are in Kreuzberg, Mitte, Neuköln and Friedrichshain. A great many of those who moved to Berlin for the cheap rent and alternative culture eventually discovered that working in cafés day-in and day-out can be quite wearing.

"We realized that just being an ordinary coworking space wasn't viable in the long run. That's why nobody *rents* here. If you're going to work here, you or your business has to be a member of Betahaus. That gives everyone a greater sense of ownership."

It also makes it possible for Betahaus to offer a whole series of members-only services that increase their members' competitive edge. Furthermore, members have access to between 60 and 70 events every month, an educational programme with around 30 workshops a month. Betahaus is a magnet for angel investors.

Today, Betahaus is a driving force behind the Berlin startup scene. But they weren't the only ones to start in 2008.

INCUBATORS: BUILDING TEAMS

"We often call 2005 and 2006 the "nuclear winter" of German entrepreneurship," Peter Borchers tells me.

Everything was dead. The IT-boom was over, and entrepreneurship became a non-issue in German politics.

"This has really changed over the past few years. Now, entrepreneurship is seen as part of the business ecosystem. There are big political events staged for entrepreneurs, and political parties are formulating policies on startups. Our previous Minister of Economic Affairs even went to Silicon Valley on a discovery trip."

Borchers has also observed a rising interest in entrepreneurship at Deutsche Telekom. He runs the company's innovation hub, called "hub:raum".

"I hope that hub:raum can strengthen Deutsche Telekom's innovation culture, and open our mind-set to the rest of the world and to innovation."

hub:raum is like a trendy institute at university. The first floor has a café, a large auditorium, and a meeting room. On the floor above is a large office space where hub:raum's staff work side-by-side with the new businesses they're investing in. 80 per cent of the applications to hub:raum have to leave via the chimney, as Borchers puts it. Roughly ten per cent receive investment, and he has a clear idea of what businesses appeal to him most.

"We mainly bet on technology businesses where we can find synergy with Deutsche Telekom. It isn't easy, but if we find a business that we can scale up and benefit from in our existing telecom products, that's very exciting for DT, commercially speaking."

And scaling is key. One of their main challenges is that teams often lack knowledge on how to build a company.

"We try to get it into their heads that they should have an idea that works on an international level. Which means we make an international business plan from day one." Although Germany is a big market, entrepreneurs cannot base their success solely on a domestic breakthrough.

"hub:raum invests between €150,000 and €300,000 in a company. In exchange, we receive ten to fifteen per cent of the stock. The founders are given office space, but the most important thing is probably that they are given access to mentors."

It is the mentors who have the skills to help businesses succeed internationally. Most of the mentors come from outside Deutsche Telekom. Nearly all of them have been successful entrepreneurs in their own right.

Although he is passionate about new technology, Borchers is also dedicated to helping build Berlin's startup scene. There hub:raum is a player, like Betahaus and a number of other incubators. The structure and thinking behind hub:raum is something he has worked on for years.

EDUCATION IS COTTONING ON TO ENTREPRENEURSHIP

On the 10th of June 2015, the Minister of Economic Affairs and Energy, Sigmar Gabriel spoke at the NOAH conference. "Germany needs a new Gründerzeit", he declared from the podium. This statement refers to the period between 1870 and 1900, when entrepreneurs made their mark on Germany. This is when companies like Daimler Motoren Gesellschaft, Bosch, AEG, Miele, and Thyssen were founded, and made German industry world leading.

Vice chancellor Gabriel feels that one obstacle to entrepreneurship is the German educational system. Schools and universities have not given students enough entrepreneurial schooling. The federal government has been aware of the problem for some time. When the "nuclear winter" was drawing to a close in 2007, politicians attempted to reinvigorate the entrepreneurial spirit in the educational system.

First, they established the entrepreneurial programme Exist III, which has created 46 projects at 100 German high schools. 60 research institutes were given money to build entrepreneurial skills and systemically teach the development and commercialization of innovative business concepts. The programme grew in 2010, when the *Bundesministerium für Wirtschaft und Energie* (BMWi: Ministry for Economic Affairs and Energy) started the amply named *Gründerland Deutschland: EXIST-Gründungskultur – Die Gründerhochschule* initiative. €46 million were set aside for German high schools competing for funding for projects that reinforced a startup culture and the entrepreneurial spirit.

In addition, 2007 saw the establishment of a grant for entrepreneurs, making it possible for them to create proper business plans for their patents. Since that time, more than 500 businesses have received support, and around 1,000 people at German universities and high schools have received help realizing their entrepreneurial projects.

"Universities have cottoned on. They realized that students could create relevant jobs for themselves. Now nearly all universities in Germany have a centre for entrepreneurship", Borchers tells us.

This commitment has led to more and more people seeing entrepreneurship as a viable first job. Max at Betahaus agrees that German universities are starting to foster a startup culture.

"I think it's very significant that universities are starting to market entrepreneurship as a third career path. Students can work for the government, for a business, or for themselves. Germany has been marked by a fear of failure, but I think that's changing."

He feels that the combination of entrepreneurship and students is invaluable to Berlin.

"It's the city with the most students in Germany. They come here to study, and now they stay because of the entrepreneurial scene. *Gründerschaft* (entrepreneurship) has become hipster-cool. Today, even the people who went to McKinsey a few years ago want to found their own business." Nevertheless, he is cautious.

"I love that universities are stimulating the growth of new businesses. But I don't like it when universities enter the private sector with public financing. That distorts competition."

80 PERCENT SUCCEED AT TU: BERLIN

"We give our businesses mentorship and a network. They also receive an Exist grant. The year they're in our business incubators, entrepreneurs are given a grant of between €2,500 and €3,000 a month. We take no shares in the company; the government doesn't allow it."

Technisches Universitet Berlin (TU Berlin: Technical University of Berlin) has a long history of launching growth-businesses, and professor Jan Kratzer at the university feels that their business incubator doesn't cause distortions. He sits in a frugally decorated office with early 80s furniture, and he is proud of the institution.

"We now have three incubators in Berlin, and produce a total of 30 startups a year."

The results are impressive. Companies that emerged from TU Berlin between 2000 and 2013 had a combined turnover of around €2.7 billion, and totalled over 20,000 employees.

"Public investment in TU's startup program is really paying off."

According to Kratzer, eight out of ten companies emerging from the incubator are still in business after five years. They only accept 30 companies a year, and a company should be founded by a team.

"Why are you so concerned that startups should be run by a team?"

"We think that teams succeed more than solo entrepreneurs. To start a technology company, you need people with different kinds of skills. You need at least one specialist. And by that I mean that you have to have an intellectual capacity in the company that cannot be outsourced. Often, you also need someone who knows industry building, how to bring ideas to life. And, of course, you need someone who knows marketing."

He pauses.

"It's good to have a woman on the team as well. Women can solve a lot of problems, but they're hard to get. Not a lot of women study to be technical engineers. A good team consists of people who complement each other."

The nuclear winter has definitely ended in Berlin. Foreigners are moving in and the economy is starting to grow. There are many states that try to copy Berlin, but in a way, Berlin has copied Estonia.

When Russian-born Gleb Tritus realized he could make money by optimizing text content on search engines, he was hooked. The young serial-entrepreneur is now addicted to one thing: starting new ventures.

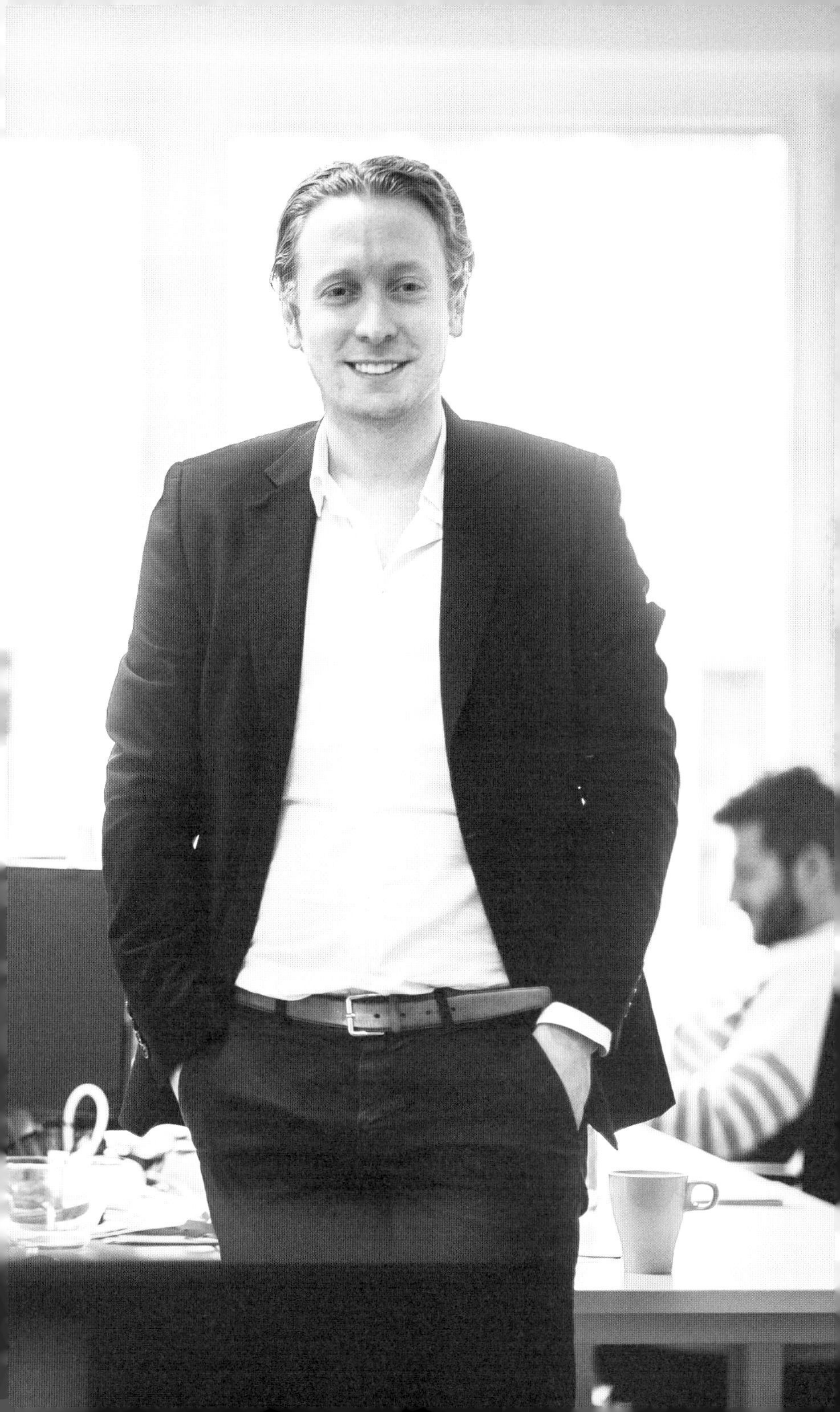

ENTREPRENEUR I

THE ENTREPRENEURIAL ADDICT
Berlin

Near "Rosenthaler Platz", literally next to the remnants of the infamous Berlin Wall, hipster-Berlin meets the German industrial machine. Welcome to Berlin's state-of-the-art coworking space called The Factory, and it's next-door-neighbour, Lufthansa Innovation Hub. Lufthansa Innovation Hub is not as shiny as its neighbour. Walking into quite an ordinary Berlin apartment building, you have to look carefully to find "Lufthansa" in handwriting taped to the wall below the quite ordinary doorbell. Inside, the hidden gem appears: It´s not the row of Lufthansa seats extracted from a retired airliner that makes the difference, it's the group of young techies working there, expanding the horizon of flying Germany.

"TECH-ING" UP THE DINOSAUR

The initiative's digital development is headed-up by Gleb Tritus. Age 31, he has already started a number of successful tech-businesses. Not only that; he has already tasted the hardship of failure. This combination gives him the potency to bring the new world into the old; his primary charge from Lufthansa HQ.

The starting point for Lufthansa's innovation hub is that every corporate business needs to become more digital. Lufthansa has 60 years of history focusing on delivering its core product of transporting people from A to B. However, providing customers a cutting-edge digital experience requires more. Many elements of today's global aviation IT-backbone pre-dates smart-phones and online check- in systems.

Global aviation is growing steadily with oil prices at a record low while legacy airlines such as Lufthansa, British Airways and Air France have to fight aggressive and agile competitors from the low-cost sector and the Middle East. In order to justify the price premium that a full-price airline operating from expensive European airports has to charge, inevitably Lufthansa has to more than outperform other airlines with regard to innovation and digitalization, explains Gleb Tritus.

Thus the young entrepreneur finds himself actually working in a legacy corporation for the first time in his life.

"QUICK AND DIRTY" PROTOTYPES

The hub has only been in operation since January 2015, continues Gleb energetically, speaking like a flying machine. Some of the team's time is spent co-operating with existing startups. The airline has a large amount of data on their customers, in addition to a huge pool of know-how from decades at the heart of the travel industry.

The airline can bring this know-how into startups such as Airbnb and the German Uber, and it works well.

Many corporations in Germany started their own innovation hubs back in 2012/13. That means that we can learn from their failures. We've found that launching "quick and dirty prototypes" – meaning very simple ideas tested in a segment of the market – gives us an advantage.

"Several entrepreneurs think they have to launch a 100 percent functioning product before they try it out. Through targeted performance marketing, we can validate our ideas in 2-3 months before perfecting the product and before we throw in more money", explains Gleb.

I can´t help thinking of Norway's fish farming industry when hearing of the hub´s way of working. It goes like this: You throw young fish into the fish farm.

You feed them with the right type of diet to grow well. You harvest. You ship to market. Gleb likes the parallel.

"We're more down to earth and more entrepreneurial than other corporate incubators. We don't throw in more than maximum €100,000 into new ventures."

FAILURE AS AN ASSET

His own "flight" as an entrepreneur started just ten years ago, when he – as a student – discovered that he could earn money optimizing text content on search engines online – so called "search engine optimization" or "SEO". Thus his first success story was with "Affaires Media" – currently employing 50 people, with customers such as Axel Springer and Deutsche Telekom. Although he's totally out of day-to-day operations, he still owns 100 percent of that company.

Later, in 2007, he started "Townster" – a rating site for restaurants and other services. This was at first a huge success, where he was able to raise a significant amount of venture capital. Then, after a few months, it totally failed. Partly the reason was that they were quite far ahead of market needs. Competitors, such as "Yelp", took off in 2010 when the market was ready for it.

Then in 2009 the cosmetic e-commerce company "poshposh" was launched. That also failed in its initial form, as it proved too hard to reach customers directly. Instead, he managed to transform it into a wholesaler and today it is a decently profitable company

– functioning in the B2B-market.¹ After that he started "todaytickets", which is a last-minute ticket provider. That was recently sold – also for a decent price.

What then, did he learn from his failures?

"My biggest failure was "Townster". At first, it was easy to raise capital. Then it failed only two months later. We had huge management problems in our founders' team. I was in a lucky position as I already owned a profitable company. One co-founder had a more challenging time though, it took him quite a while to recover."

"I think I was in a state of depression for about six months. I was actually close to seeing a doctor. I had to lay off 35 people. We had bad press. We were called the "high fliers" of the Cologne startup scene. I burnt some bridges with some well-known business angels. But – I was lucky – as I started to earn money again in new ways, I got over it. If I had not – I think it would have been another game."

He has also learnt that expanding a company is the hardest bit.

"Scaling-up was definitely the hardest part. It is extremely hard to find the right talent with the right skills. Germany has strict immigration laws and it is hard to find tech-personnel and marketing personnel. The war for talent has never been harder and it is still a problem."

This know-how was an asset for Lufthansa.

---

1   "Business-to-business", meaning serving other businesses which again serve consumers.

"The lessons learned through both success and failure were relevant to what they wanted to establish in the Innovation Hub. In Germany, there is still the culture that you easily burn yourself and your name if you've failed big time. We're still far from the American way, where failure really is seen as an asset", explains Gleb.

He 'is not quite hyperactive: He comes across as energetic yet calm. Do these traits run in his blood? Is he a natural born entrepreneur?

"My parents are in some ways entrepreneurs. They run a symphony orchestra in Cologne. It includes the same traits: You pay your people. You need to be good at sales. You work on the business development and on advertisement. Some aspects of running a business, I definitely learnt from them."

SEARCHING FOR A WAY TO STANDARDIZE BUILDING SUCCESSFUL STARTUPS

Now he is definitely addicted to starting new ventures. He's lived through total failure and great success. He is still trying to crack the systematic way of starting a business that can be repeated, to standardize building a growing company. Tritus thinks this kind of reasoning is an asset for Germany. Many other venture environments fail in developing systematic ways of growing companies. Every new trial is a new trial.

"My big question is: How can we standardize this? How can we reduce the risk? You can't standardize everything, but many parts of the journey for new companies are really the same", explains Gleb.

I wonder – is this starting to be his life mission? It makes sense that Lufthansa wanted him on board. In the environment of Berlin founders, many – like him – are still young but already have the experience of starting and failing and succeeding, each two or three times. The Berlin scene has grown to some maturity. Hyped as it may still be - something is happening.

Gleb's vision can't be to "fly" with Lufthansa forever. He seems too impatient to stay for life. And indeed he admits he must start his own business again sometime in the future. But for now, his short-term aim is to make the Lufthansa Innovation Hub profitable. For the airline to want to keep it going, that has to be achieved in the next 1-2 years.

"I do not see myself in a corporate in the long-term as I got the «entrepreneurial bug» at an early stage. However, I do see myself bringing value to Lufthansa Group at this time and I also get back a lot of value in terms of reconnecting with knowledge and people in the «old economy». Both sides can definitely profit from each other and I can recommend this experience sincerely to other entrepreneurs."

FACTS ABOUT GLEB TRITUS:

NAME: Gleb Tritus, Co-Creator & Director of Venture Development at Lufthansa Innovation Hub, Berlin.

"I think I was in a state of depression for about six months. I was actually close to seeing a doctor. I had to lay off 35 people.

BORN: 1984, by parents who run a professional symphony orchestra in Cologne.
FROM: Yekatarinaburg, Russia (grew up in Germany). Education: Bachelor of Arts (B.A.), International Business, Cologne Business School.

What would you do if you were Prime Minister: I would speed up the process of maturing the venture capital scene in Germany. The business angel community especially in Berlin is like a huge construction site, and they lack the right incentives to invest. That would make it easier to invest the first 500,000 Euros, as this seed money is the most challenging to find.

What is the best thing about being an entrepreneur in Berlin: It is being in the right place at the right time. Now, in 2015, everything we lacked only five years ago is in place. There is far more venture capital here now, and the entrepreneurial spirit is by far stronger. The factors are coming together in Berlin.

What is the worst thing about being an entrepreneur in Berlin: The worst thing is that the Berlin-scene is totally overhyped. People think Berlin is like Hollywood for startups, and think one can become a millionaire overnight. We are maturing here – but there is still a way to go.

THREE GOLDEN TIPS FOR YOUNG ENTREPRENEURS:

1. Build the right team. Build the right team. And build the right team. A good team can make something out of a bad idea, but a bad team can destroy even the best idea. This is very applicable to everyone.
2. Build measures to learn from your journey at once. "Fail fast". In 2015 we have the tools to do so. Use the right analytical tools. It is very important to "smoke test" ideas in the market without investing real value in them too early.
3. Produce numbers. Prove that your idea has traction for at least three months before you approach a Venture Capitalist!

"My big question is: How can we standardize this? How can we reduce the risk? You can't standardize everything, but many parts of the journey for new companies are really the same"

CHAPTER 2
THE STARTUP STATE
Estonia

> The Estonian government may have understood before anyone else that technology could make the country wealthy. After "Skype" and "Transfer Wise" became breakthrough hits it was obvious to everyone.

35 Norwegians are eating lunch. Not that odd, as things go – you might see the same in any number of cafeterias in Norway on a given day. Only this isn't Norway, it's Tallinn. The lunch guests represent Norwegian companies and have just arrived in town. Norwegian companies send people to Tallinn fairly often. Estonia is the biggest supplier of pre-fab housing in Norway, DNB has a sizeable presence in Tallinn, and Rimi is the biggest supermarket chain in the country. And it isn't just Norwegian companies with footprints in Estonia, Swedish companies abound, as do the Danes.

For Scandinavian companies the Baltics might almost be described as a wild-wild-west, the labour

This page is sponsored by Intro Church, Sandnes

market is not very regulated, taxes are low, and the price of labour is cheap. Since the fall of the Soviet Union no European country has grown as fast as Estonia, and that growth is continuing. French economists at CETII believe that within ten years, Estonia's gross national product per capita will be at the same level as the Nordic countries.

The 35 Norwegians are interested in growth, but neither pre-fab housing nor groceries are their specialities. They are in Estonia for Innovation Norway's conference, "Green IT – Norway-Estonia Cooperation Seminar". People are talking about whether Russia is a threat to Estonia, if the upturn in the Estonian economy will keep going, but first and foremost the conversations are about cooperation with Estonian companies.

Tallinn is all about IT, not least this week, as "Tallinn ICT Week" kicks off. And it's not just Scandinavians travelling to Tallinn. It would be an exaggeration to say that everyone goes to Tallinn nowadays, but many do, including 500 Germans from German industrial corporations.

Let's not forget the British. The British are everywhere in Tallinn. And they all want to talk IT. And this is of course not without reason: Little Estonia is a computing giant.

OUT OF ESTONIA

Kari Maripuu runs the company Brightspark. I'm meeting him at a reception at the Norwegian embassy in Tallinn. Like all startups in Estonia Maripuu is also looking for new partners.

"I have been in software since I was 16", he says.

In the year 2000 he started an IT-company in a small town called Parno. Two years later he was nearly bankrupt. Parno was a little city with few customers, however the experience helped him find a job with two foreign IT companies in Estonia: IBM and TeliaSonera.

"After five years I wanted to do something for myself. My idea was to create a company that develops concepts for clients. That way we don't have to bill programming hours, we can just create the concept and take a share of the proceeds."

Their first big job was in e-commerce. It involved developing a betting page for horse racing in Estonia. At that time Maripuu made a choice, he no longer wanted to work solely towards the Estonian market. The Estonian market was too small, and not least, there was heavy competition. It was hard to make money. Maripuu would rather have a fraction of the international market than be a dominant player in Estonia.

His first international customer was a Ferrari salesman in Italy.

"They were sitting on an old database of Ferrari-owners. We made a platform for buying and selling cars. That site won us a development award."

After that experience he got in touch with Enterprise Estonia, who in turn put him in touch with the Norwegian engineering company Asplan Viak.

This page is sponsored by Arttu Makipaa, Brussels

Together they are developing a database to measure how power can be efficiently distributed in new buildings. He received a €350,000 grant to develop the database, which enabled Brightspark to hire. Since then, Brightspark has developed a digital logistics database to handle shipping packages in the United States and Great Britain. Today they are working with an English brokerage to create a portal to sell traded stocks online.

"We can't risk building our own brand. That would make us dependent on selling one product. Now, we're able to develop many concepts", he explains.

ROLE MODELS

"It's businesses that aim for international success with new technology and their own brands that Technopol wishes to develop", says Triin Mahlakõiv.

Technopol is an incubator like Lufthansa Innovation Hub and hub:raum. It is the only technology-based incubator in the Baltics. Director Triin Mahlakõiv is optimistic, as increasing numbers of Estonian startups are developing their own brands.

"Skype was, until Microsoft bought the company, the role model for the Estonian startup scene. After the company was sold, many former employees there started their own businesses."

Skype gave many Estonians experience on how to create an international startup. This is the exact kind of role model that has been missing from the startup scene in many countries. Currently TransferWise may be the most important source of inspiration for young startups. The Estonian startup giant has over 150 employees in Tallinn alone, and is trying to attract smart people from the Estonian IT-scene.

"Technopol is a little different from most other European incubators because our programme is more like an accelerator, and because we require a prototype from our members."

As is the case for incubators in Berlin, startups ought to have at least two founders; one with technological competence and one business-developer. Mahlakõiv explains that their mentor team decides which startups get accepted. They base their calls on whether they think it's possible to scale the concept internationally and therefore want to work with it. Technopol believes that businesses at an early stage of development may benefit from being in the incubator for up to three months. That's the time they need to find new mentors.

The approach delivers results. When Mahlakõiv looks for investments abroad, she often receives praise.

"We're often told that our startups actually solve real problems, they are not just a fancy concept."

She highlights the company Safetoact, which produces artificial kidneys for doctors to practice on. This could potentially lead to small-scale industrial production. And the reason is that it's based on a solid prototype, not just an idea.

"Prototyping is expensive, that's why we started the Prototron foundation. The foundation can provide businesses with a development grant up to €20,000. Swedbank donated the money. During the last round, Prototron received 200 applications and gave four of them development support."

The incubator is located just outside the town centre in a business park that could be mistaken for a technology university campus. Its office space consists of little cubicles for the startups and a large common area. The most striking thing about the common area is that it's full of advertising for British tax and corporate law.

Mahlakõiv underscores that their startups also view Germany and the U.S. as interesting markets, but as London has numerous investors and a fertile startup ecosystem, many prefer the UK as their first international market. Strong connections have obviously developed between the Estonian and British startup communities.

BRINGING TOGETHER A TEAM

As I entered the kitchen at Garage48, another focal point in Tallinn's startup scene, I stared at a huge Union Jack on the wall. Jane Muts smiles, telling me that Garage48 is an NGO.

"We need sponsors and partners to survive. The British embassy gave us some money, but when they visited and saw our kitchen wall, which was quite ugly, they asked, "You wouldn't like a flag for this wall, would you? We have rather a large one." The Brits like to display their flag," says Muts.

Ragnar Sass, Martin Villig and Jüri Kaljundi started HUB in 2010. It was a spin-off from the Garage 48 Foundation. Their core business is arranging *hackathons*, events at which programmers and software-developers cooperate with other professions to solve a specific problem. The themes for the events in Tallinn have included "hardware and art" and "green technology."

She points out that many young people have ideas, but few of them know how to implement them. Others have relevant experience, but few ideas. As both hub:raum and TU – Berlin emphasized, building the right team is pivotal in order to grow a successful company. If everything works out well, hackathons can bring good teams together. When a hackathon is over, roughly 50 percent of the teams continue to launch startups.

"After the hackathon, they often have a prototype, which means they can go to accelerators in search of money. Some also apply for funding from Prototron."

"You can just look at our Wall of Fame, which includes the companies TransferWise, Lingvist and Guardtime."

SMALL TOWN, DIGITAL STATE

One reason for Tallinn's success, according to Muts, is that it's quite a small town.

"It's easy to cooperate with institutions here. Most of them know each other. If you have a good idea and a prototype, it's fairly easy to get to pitch it to a bank manager."

And the Estonian government, says Mahlakõiv, has understood the value of cooperation and entrepreneurship. That is why tax laws are very simple. The country has a flat tax rate and companies don't pay corporate tax. Only dividends are taxed. Starting a company takes 15 minutes online. It's obvious that when the establishment facilitates entrepreneurship in this way, it ripples outward. Today, Estonia has the highest number of startups per capita in Europe.

"The government has been very positive to new technology. They have cooperated with private startups to renew the public sector," Mahlakõiv explains.

IT-entrepreneurs made it possible for Estonian authorities be the first to digitalize not only public administration, but banking as well. With a single ID-card, you have access to all public information, including health and education, but also your own bank account.

Rainer Kattel is a professor of innovation at the Technical University in Tallinn. He tells me that Estonia is probably the world leader in electronic public administration.

"We take it for granted that all official correspondence takes place digitally. Our electronic tax filing and Inland Revenue are a shining success."

Kattel says that their success is due to the cooperation between the state, entrepreneurs, the banking sector and telecoms, as Estonia went from Soviet to modern banking.

He explains that the banks wanted to start electronic banking and the telecom-companies wanted to put down new cables. So, they convinced the state to cooperate with them, and together they put together a digital framework for bank, government, and telecommunications. The business sector helped the government because their interests aligned.

The idea seems captivatingly simple, but also like every hacker's dream. He'd be able to steal a person's identity, access their bank account and health records. The Estonians, however, feel that they have solved this problem. Their system is called X-Road, and has had little trouble with hackers.

The startup company Guardtime developed X-Road. Data security was a concern from day one, and they decided that instead of storing everything in a central database, all information should be stored locally using so-called block chain technology. In addition, everyone with access must approve all changes to the data stored. The consequence is that hacking attempts are discovered right away – which reduces the temptation.

"The fact that X-Road not only works, but is a secure system makes this a great success," says Kattel.

This is why not only companies travel to Estonia to cooperate, bureaucrats are also starting to come in droves. In 2015, Finland even went so far as to buy a licence for X-Road. The system will be used when the Finns digitalize their public sector.

Estonians are happy to tell this story: First, the Estonian IT-industry started outsourcing to international companies. Then they started founding international computer companies, and now the state exports their IT-solutions.

ATTRACTING FOREIGN INTEREST

Success in the Estonian IT-sector is the reason that the British are active on the startup scene in Tallinn, that Norwegian businesses are travelling to Estonia to find IT-partners, and why DIHK has a strong presence during Tallinn's ICT Week. It has also contributed to Estonia having the strongest growth in Europe since the fall of the Soviet Union.

In 2015 Estonia launched "e-citizenship". Not only Estonians will benefit from the country's system. Wherever you live, you can start a company, create a bank account and sign public papers online in Estonia. They are looking for more entrepreneurs.

"Half our members are foreign. They come from Romania, Italy, Spain, France and Finland. Some of them moved to Tallinn because of a relationship while others continue to live here after their studies. In the last few years more and more people have come to start companies here. It's easy to start up here; so many come to avoid regulations. That particularly applies to start-ups from southern Europe and France," explains Jane Muts.

She feels that with e-citizenship, even more people will want to start a business in Estonia.

In Enterprise Estonia, the largest Estonian employers' organization, head of communications Maarja Loorentz is also positive about e-citizenship.

"It's easy to apply for e-citizenship, which means you can establish an Estonian business from India, the United States or Europe. Creating a bank account isn't as simple yet, but we're working on it."

Whether this will lead to many foreigners starting Estonian businesses in order to avoid their home countries' bureaucracies remains to be seen.

However Mahlakõiv at Technopol has noticed great interest, Technopol have had a number of enquiries from people in Asia about e-citizenship. Both investors and companies see it as an interesting way to enter the European market. Whatever the case, Estonia's IT sector has at least contributed to giving the country a stronger position in Europe.

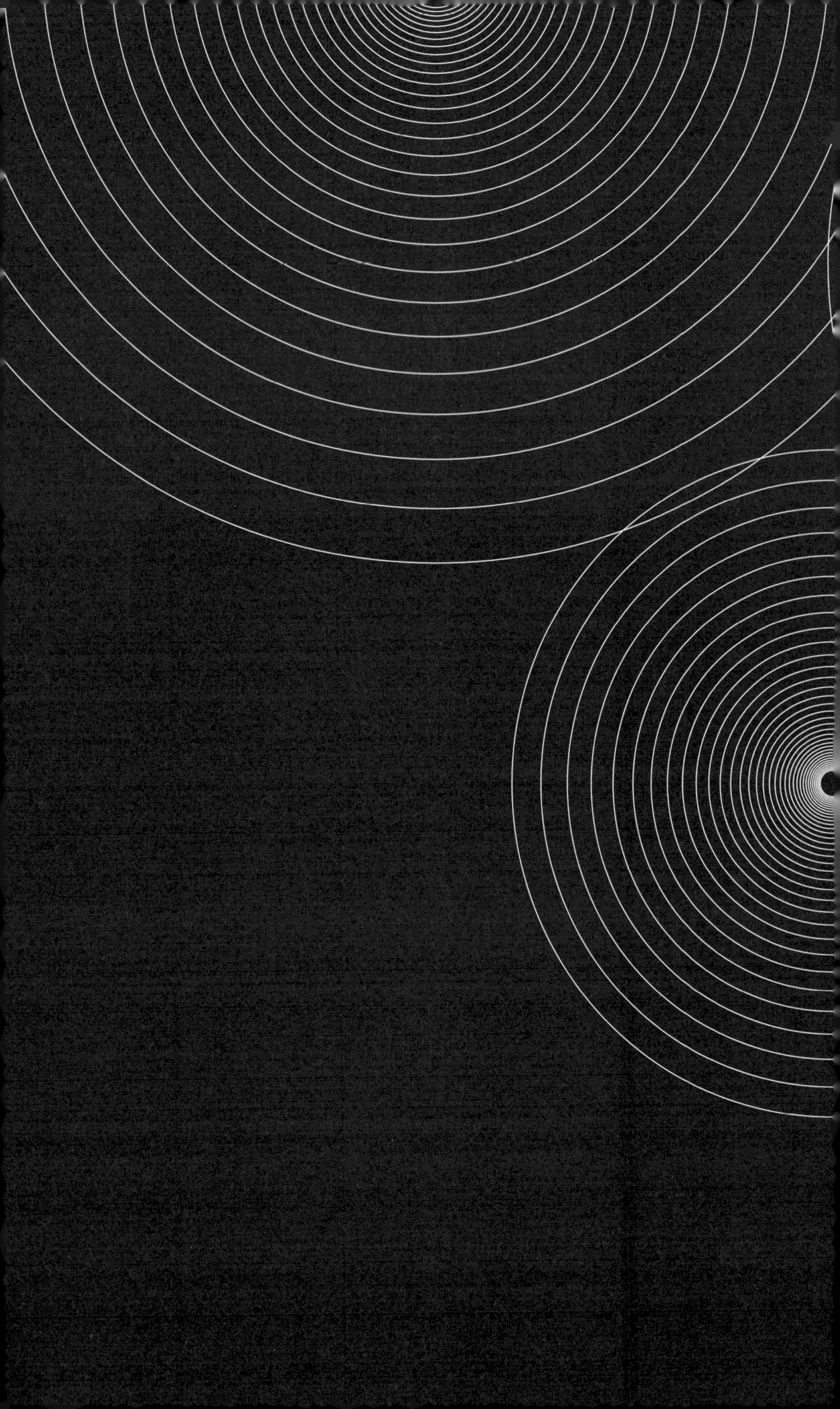

Part 2: FROM CONCEPT TO INDUSTRY?

The fourth industrial revolution is changing the business world. Many cities try to adapt and attract talented foreigners. In Lisbon, an entrepreneur is trying to revolutionize logistics and in Oslo it is becoming cheaper to make prototypes.

CHAPTER 3
THE SEEDS OF SUCCESS
Lisbon

> The entrepreneurs of Lisbon have a dream: that their city will become the California of Europe.

Lisbon is comfortable. The October climate is nice and warm, the thermometer reads 20 degrees. I have just enjoyed a light breakfast consisting of a sandwich, a small nata pastry and a coffee on my way to meet Carlos Neto. He works at Portugal Ventures.

As I was paying my €7 for breakfast I thought for the first time that day; *I should move here*. Of course I'd also had that thought when I paid for my shellfish dinner the previous evening. And now, wandering in the sun along the Atlantic on my way to the underground station Chiado/Baixa, I find myself thinking it again.

There may be few monuments in Lisbon, but the city is nevertheless a baroque adventure. Walking down the Rua Augusta in the central district Baixa, one looks through a large portal. This is the triumphal arch from the end of the 1700s, radiating former greatness. At the time Lisbon was the capital of a kingdom that included

Brazil. The way the triumphal arch draws the eye can safely be called long-term city planning. Lisbon also has medieval sites to see. Particularly worthwhile is the castle Castelo de São Jorge, conquered by the Reconquista in 1147, looming over the baroque city centre.

In addition there is something for nostalgics. I almost couldn't believe my eyes when I saw the city-trams. They look just like the 1940s. As a consequence of the monuments, pleasant climate and low prices there are a lot of tourists in Lisbon. Many of them roll in groups up to the castle on Segways. I walk around thinking; *they were on to something once, the Portuguese*. But today nearly everything is inherited from the past. The trams, the buildings and the tourists are old, and Lisbon is the capital of one of Europe's poorest nations. And in contrast to Spain, the financial crisis isn't the problem.

Already in 2006, economic growth was at 1.3 percent – the lowest in Europe. In the 2000s, the Czech Republic, Malta and Slovenia all passed Portugal in GDP per capita. Today, Slovakia and even the Seychelles have surpassed the old colonial power. The Portuguese economy is roughly half the size of Spain's per capita, and little more than a third of Germany's.

This is partly due to poor levels of education. Only 67 per cent of the workforce has completed primary school. Although Lisbon is attractive, the real narrative is that 10,000 people have left Portugal every month since 2009.

This page is sponsored by Elias El Makdessi, Beirut

However that is not the whole story. A new narrative is emerging. As prices dropped, a few artists and galleries started doing quite well. They established a winning business model: Live in low-cost Lisbon, and sell your art in the in the far more prosperous northern Europe. That sounds familiar – that sounds like Berlin.

Simultaneously the Portuguese political class were painfully aware of the country's problems. Like Berlin and Tallinn, they recognised the need to build an ecosystem for enhancing entrepreneurship. In 2012 they merged all public efforts to invest in startups. The result was Portugal Ventures. The mayor of Lisbon knew of Berlin's burgeoning economic growth and realized that he had to do something to create more jobs in the city. Part of the remedy was the business incubator Startup Lisboa, which opened its doors in 2011.

THE CALIFORNIA OF EUROPE

I find Portugal Ventures' offices in a high-rise in the modern part of Lisbon. Carlos Neto explains that a lot of people are still leaving Portugal, but they're not the people who contribute to economic growth.

"The people leaving Portugal are educated, but have lost their jobs. These might be journalists, consultants, or people in international relations. They want to extend their careers and make a decent wage."

That is why they go abroad. However, Neto is sure that some of them will return. Immediately after graduating, few have the experience to start a company. In

Great Britain and Germany ambitious people are given responsibility more quickly than in Portugal, which prevents a brain drain. However, when his countrymen have acquired some knowledge, Neto thinks that many will return and start companies based on what they've learned.

He believes the startup scene in Lisbon has evolved over the past four years. An entrepreneur can find cheap office space and there are many coworking spaces around town. Lisbon is actually very cost friendly.

"Compared with Germany, Great Britain and Scandinavia, the price of labour is inexpensive."

It is almost tempting to call Lisbon the new Berlin. At least the city's conditions have captured the interest of startups and investors from the United States, Scandinavia and Germany.

"And there is a lot of sun here! That's one of the reasons entrepreneurs come. Good weather means that young entrepreneurs can have a good time in the city, while at the same time, the low prices mean that they can focus on building their business."

At Portugal Ventures they've noticed many foreigners moving to Lisbon to join the startup adventure.

"The dream is that Portugal can become a European California. Portuguese are very interested in technology. We are far to the west, we've got the weather, and actually, we even have a bridge that looks a little like the Golden Gate."

This page is sponsored by Rayan Jireh, Athens

Neto has a twinkle in his eye. He's about to be serious. Of course he knows that Portugal can't become another Silicon Valley, but his point is that conditions are favourable for growth in Portugal. It's easy to start a company under the programme "Company Now". The paperwork is simple. Moreover you can pay your taxes directly online. Neto thinks that all the changes in administration and the city's positive attitude is due to Portugal receiving a bit of a shock.

"I think the financial crisis has been a real motivator."

THE FINEST GENERATION

Those who want a comfortable existence set up their life in the centre of Lisbon. That's where all the houses with beautifully tiled walls are situated. You'll find cafés and bars there. It's only three minutes from the beach. This is also where you'll find Startup Lisboa.

"Becoming the test bed of Europe isn't just a dream – we *could* actually be just that," says Bruno Gomes.

He believes Lisbon has special advantages. They're in the same time zone as London and the airport is close to the city centre. It's easy to get in and out.

Gomes, like Neto, highlights the fine weather and pleasant environment. You can work hard until three o'clock, have a few hours of surfing and lunch at the beach, and then start to work again at six. That puts you in the office during both European and American business hours. But his main point is the low prices, multiple

You can work hard until three o'clock, have a few hours of surfing and lunch at the beach, and then start to work again at six. That puts you in the office during both European and American business hours.

incubators and abundance of mentors for startups. In short, Gomes feels that Lisbon has a smoothly functioning ecosystem.

People who want to start a business in London quickly discover the competitive nature of the market. Neither space nor labour is cheap in London. In Lisbon, the quality is the same.

"The last few years, we've created the finest generation of Portuguese ever, but they couldn't find work. So they moved abroad, but now they're coming back to start their own companies here."

Gomes feels that this "finest generation" of Portuguese is what makes Lisbon unique. For startups, the war for talent isn't as tough as it is in Berlin or London.

Yet, emigration represents a problem.

"We need more people who start businesses while they're at university. It's not true that you need to work for several years before starting on your own," says Gomes.

Joana Mendonca, with Nova Business School (NBS), echoes these words. As several universities in Portugal have, NBS has started a programme to stimulate more young entrepreneurs. Mendonca is heading up a programme called "Nova Entrepreneurship Office".

"Really, we're a people who don't like to take risks. The last few years, a lot of infrastructure has been created. That gives the impression that there are a lot of entrepreneurs here, but it wasn't really until 2010 that most people thought of going into business for themselves."

Rui Paulo Figuiredo is a member of parliament for the Socialist Party. He also feels that Portugal has had a mentality problem.

"A lot of business people, students, and workers are very close to the state. They look to the government or to local authorities to solve their problems. As students graduate they try to find permanent employment, preferably in the public sector."

Figuiredo thinks that it is only in the last few years that this has started to change. Today young Portuguese are both more internationally and business oriented.

"The financial crisis has probably contributed to this change," he says, "because people change their opinions based on migration and unemployment. The young people of today have given up hope that the government can solve all their problems."

Neto at Portugal Ventures agrees.

"People want to change the system now. They want to see disruptive change."

"In Europe, including Portugal, the government has believed that old companies like Nestlé, Lego, and Nokia can solve unemployment issues. As a consequence, Europe has generated few new companies that have changed the continent and created new jobs – including jobs for people with little education. The majority of new jobs from the startup sector are still for well educated people," claims Neto.

Mendonca at NBS shares Neto's analysis.

"Those who are born in the eighties, who were young in 2008, they are the ones starting new companies."

Until recently the startup scene consisted almost exclusively of technology companies. Now startups are also fusing with and renewing traditional businesses. The rising focus on retail was probably a spin-off from the tourist trade, as most businesses in Portugal outside the technology sector are tied to tourism. This kind of scaling is important for the country.

"90 per cent of our businesses are small companies. We've always had a tradition of running our own businesses. Now those small businesses are starting to think about innovation, and they realise the need to renew themselves in order to survive. They understand that the corner store must grow and become something larger. The whole economy is changing."

The government has actually started to pay entrepreneurs to employ people. If you employ an intern you can get as much as 80 per cent of their salary covered. This helps companies expand faster, while simultaneously reducing unemployment.

One example is "Zaask" – a platform that helps you find tradesmen. Today, all sorts of services can be found there, even if you're looking for a DJ for a party. Another company is "Academia de Codigo", which teaches unemployed people to code. Mendonca explains that not all these businesses are easy to scale up. The ones that succeed have a clear concept.

"Cheak by Choice have been very successful. Not to mention Nata – a small neighbourhood coffee chain that sells little egg pastries. In 12 years they have expanded to 12 countries."

FROM CONCEPT TO INDUSTRY

The chain Nata only sells nata and coffee. Currently the company is starting cafés all over Europe. One of the latest outlets to be opened is in Torggata in Oslo. The café is similar to countless other cafes in Lisbon, but it has something the others lack, a clear concept.

It's easy to compare the concept economy with contemporary art. In Oslo the Astrup Fearnley Museum recently unveiled the exhibition *A Love Story*. The collection belongs to polar explorer and adventurer Erling Kagge. The museum and Kagge have filled the building with pieces intended to provoke. In the middle of the floor was a banana peel that Kagge supposedly bought for a handsome sum. On the first floor is the receipt from a grocery store, the common denominator being that all the products are white. Kagge, in effect, bought a "license" to buy white products at stores from the artist. The point is, for a certain number of visitors to cry out, "Is this art?"

The pieces can be categorised as concept art. They can be characterised as idea-based artistic work, in the sense that the idea behind the art is judged more important than the craftsmanship or visual finish. An observer is supposed to think; *this is a cool design*, *this conveys*

This bage is sponsored by www.base-group.co.uk

a strong message, or *this is madness!* – And hopefully; *I want this!* Chevrolet played with this concept in the 50s when they made cars with a lot of chrome, strong colours, and retractable roofs. The message was obvious; *Eye it. Try it. Buy it.*

This method of creating art is in strong contrast to paintings of artists such as Hans Gude (1825 – 1903). Hans Gude was technically brilliant. For hours he would sit along the coast of Wales, the lakes of Bavaria, or by the Oslo fjord studying the play of light on the water, or how ships and boats broke up the horizon. Then he would go back to his studio and compose a painting. The work was a carefully thought out piece of craftsmanship.

The ideas behind the pictures were not revolutionary, it was all about his technique. If one looks for a parallel, it's easy to think of Audi's slogan: "Vorsprung durch technick". Anyone looking at an Audi is supposed to be left thinking; *Wow. It can't be done better. I want this car.*

Another way of looking at new products is that they either have to be fit or sexy. That is the difference between Skype, Spotify, X-Road and Unilabs, Style in a Box, and Foodora. Style in a Box and Foodora are quite cool concepts, but the companies are working from a platform offering a service and using existing technology. You could find small apartments online before Unilabs was founded, and you could have food delivered from good restaurants before Foodora arrived, but these new companies have a cooler concept. For the companies using existing technology to offer a product, the strength of the concept is the deciding factor

These companies are different from the first category, which are based on new technology. Before Spotify, most people could not stream music legally. Before Skype we could not have voice conversations over the Internet, and before X-Road all communication with banks and the public sector was paper-based.

Neither Skype nor X-Road comes across as cool. The main thing is that they work. One of Portugal's fastest growing companies is called Wide Scope. Wide Scope is attempting to revolutionise a big industry: the logistics industry. It isn't super-sexy, but it is based on new technology and very efficient.

From a functional and modest Lisbon office, mathematician Filipe Carvalho is growing one of Portugal's most successful IT startups. Success didn't come easy for this humble Portuguese and his co-founding wife.

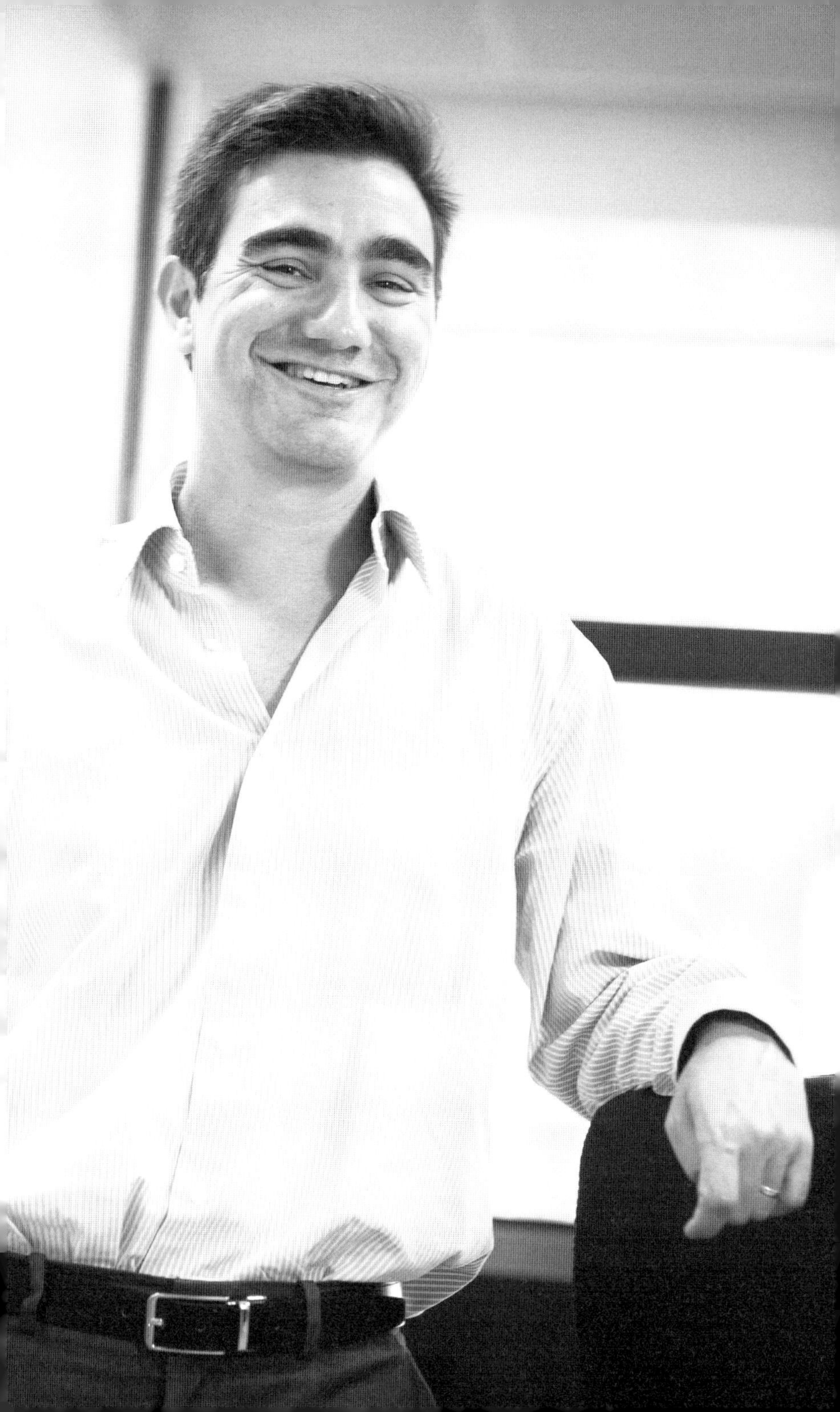

ENTREPRENEUR 2

THE PERSISTENT LOGISTICS EXPERT

Lisbon

Wide Scope is among Portugal's top ten growth companies and according to Deloitte (2012) among the "technology fast 500" in Europe, the Middle East and Africa. This is due to top revenue growth rates over recent years. They currently employ 35 people.

We meet Filipe in his 7th floor office in Lisbon's uptown business district. The location is good but there is little flashy about Wide Scope's founder and CEO. Even though he is suited up and fashionably dressed like most of Lisbon's business community, he obviously does not like bragging about himself. This makes him very likeable to a north-European author with puritan roots.

His humble appearance does signify one thing though: Filipe is all about quality. This is probably why his company is part of a European Commission-initiated research consortium propelling R&D in the fields of distribution, logistics and warehouse management.

Filipe is playing with the big fish: PSA Peugeot Citroen, Fiat, The Swedish Institute for Computer Science and many more research universities across Europe.

CUTTING COSTS, LOWERING EMISSIONS

What Wide Scope does so well that boosts their sales is to help transportation, manufacturing and medical industries substantially cut costs as well as environmental emissions. Sometimes they lower a company's production costs by as much as 20 percent. No wonder Wide Scope is expanding, currently with offices in Australia and Turkey in addition to the Portuguese headquarters.

Although seemingly mundane and usually hidden to consumers, logistics planning in transportation and manufacturing is an art for the mathematically gifted. Historically it has required in-depth planning and extensive use of project planning tools, Gantt charts and engineering analytical capabilities.

Despite this, getting the "how much" in "what sequence" or "transport where-to" and by "the fastest route" has not always been easy. In fact, when logistics go wrong, slashing production has often been the only option for the manufacturer. Not anymore. With the past decade's high-tech revolution, digitization of logistics planning becomes smarter, easier and more cost-effective – with the right software. In this market Portugal's Wide Scope is a rising star.

Their core products are "Routyn", their state of the art web-based route planning tool, and "Wide Scope scheduler" where manufacturers can plan and schedule production lines, extraordinary deliveries and use of resources. However, there are dozens of such software products available, what makes Wide Scope stand out from the crowd is their method of implementing their software with new customers, tailoring the software to customers' needs.

Together with Ana, his wife, Filipe started the company straight out of university, with the basic idea of inseminating mathematics into Portugal's business world. They knew it could improve the operation of companies in a sector where they didn't see mathematics well used. However they had to create the formula for it themselves.

"The effort did not pay off at all the first few years. We had no professional experience, no products to sell – we were just willing to create something new", explains Carvalho.

"We made absolutely no money the first year! I remember buying a newspaper at one point, thinking the guy behind the counter had more income then we had! It was really harsh."

However he shows no signs of regret, yet we sense from his personality that success didn't come easily, it was a result of persistence.

PURSUING ONESELF

Persistence he must have inherited from his forefathers. In a country emerging from decades of dictatorship, his talent and his motivation to create something new has charged him with the duty of re-discovering Portugal's hidden entrepreneurial energy.

"We didn't give up. We believed we could make a change and we needed to find our way. I am not trying to say that persistence always leads to success. I hate the idea that entrepreneurship always entails suffering – I don't think it always does or that it helps anyone if I say so." He would rather focus on the positive potential of succeeding.

So, instead of elaborating on the hardships, he often speaks to students about pursuing oneself. There is more to life than applying for poorly paid jobs with existing companies or the state. Filipe always wanted to do something different and new. He never saw himself doing a standard job.

Instead he found his drive in improving others' lives and filling a gap between needs in the market and existing ways of working. His skill as a mathematician was going to be the tool.

"The turn from bad to better for our company did not come from one year to another. The first issue we had to solve was the fact that we had no funding."

Not even their parents could help, so they started from their home.

"This is the really interesting part. We had to bootstrap. What that meant was that we had to use our skills on something else than our core business idea to be able to pay the bills. We built our long-term dream on the side. So we developed websites and through that made enough money to allow us to create the software we really wanted to build."

After a few years of bootstrapping, they had managed to develop their first software program. It was a product that improved scheduling for factories. After the product was launched, their product range grew. What they found to be their competitive advantage was their ability to significantly improve their customer's strategy and company culture.

Thus they are not merely selling products. They literally guide large and often "old" companies through a process of change, coming out leaner and more efficient.

"Being the cheapest is something I absolutely don't advise. Occupy your own space in a market. It's all about how you perform a chain of activities in comparison to competitors. It is a set of activities that we do that differentiates us. That's how – I believe – you create a competitive advantage."

"Being the cheapest is something I absolutely don't advise. Occupy your own space in a market. It's all about how you perform a chain of activities in comparison to competitors.

The commercial process in Wide Scope's market would usually be to present software for customers. Then they're allowed to try it for 15 days. Then one presents the price and hopefully there is a purchase.

"We work the other way around. We say to a potential customer: "We can see that you have a potential to cut the cost substantially in your operations. May we solve your problem?" Then we load their data and do all the consulting necessary."

He explains that there is no charge or commitment upfront.

"Once we've done the job and show them we can cut their cost with as much as 20 percent, they often want to buy our product and services. This way, we beat our competitors as they usually don´t get a chance to show their systems to their prospects in the first place."

THE SEARCH FOR SKILLS

The Carvalhos and Wide Scope found their business model – and it worked. Scaling up the company wasn't easy either. The systems they´ve developed take a lot of effort to implement in a business operation. The biggest challenge was to find the right employees who had knowledge of customers' needs and the business process in relation to Wide Scope's systems and methods.

"This is what keeps us from growing at a faster pace."

Although the tax structure in Portugal in the eyes of most entrepreneurs is bad, this is not the key factor.

Complaining about it does no good, he says. Instead, he's globalizing to find new skills and new markets.

New offices in Turkey and Australia recently opened. The vision is to change how the world of logistics operates. They want to see every customer they work with change the way they operate and thus expend less fuel. This will also help the economy turn greener faster – not a bad by-product to making good money!

Looking back on the journey, there have been failures and setbacks on the way. In Portugal, as elsewhere, Carvalho thinks the fear of failure is the major obstacle for most entrepreneurs, including himself. His main nightmare has been to be copied by competitors with larger resources who can scale faster than him.

"I think tech is a key player in any market today. It will keep growing in the years to come, and in the area of logistics, we will see more and more interconnected supply chains. A supplier in China is able to sell to a customer in the streets of Stockholm or London. I also think we will see more collaborative activity. Tech is serving as the tool for improving this."

He is excited about the possibilities. Activities that were extremely expensive to execute before, are quite viable today.

RED-TAPE AND BRAIN DRAIN

Carvalho insists on not complaining, but not touching on Portugal's infamous tax system would be to omit the environment entrepreneurs face in the country.

"Yes. Of course we can always complain until the taxes are zero. The instability of the tax structures is the biggest challenge. You hire someone the first year – then the next year the government either increases taxes for the employee or on the company's side. This is bad for us on both sides of the coin. We don't want you to earn less, so we have to compensate for the taxation."

At least he finally complains a bit, pointing out that this is absolutely illegal according to EU-agreements. Double-taxation has been common – and even triple taxation of goods and services has occurred.

Red-tape has fortunately diminished in Portugal over the years. In less than an hour, one can register a new company and fewer permits are needed than before. But, if one is in the service sector such as running a restaurant, different types of inspections by all sorts of agencies still occur. This is a type of indirect taxation that slows Portugal's growth, and it makes it harder for new businesses to operate.

For the tech sector, it is easier. If one talks about entrepreneurship in Portugal – as in many places - one thinks of the tech sector. However Carvalho says his country needs more than that. Not everyone has the capability to start high-tech based operations, and for unemployment to fall, Portugal needs a range of start-ups in several sectors.

"Another challenge we face in Portugal is the brain drain that has been going on since the financial crisis hit us in 2008. Many smart people found few opportunities to grow their careers, and some not even to enter the business. They felt they had to leave."

But he does see light at the end of the tunnel. Portuguese universities are both preparing their students for entrepreneurship in new ways, and to better tackle the challenges Portugal face. They will supply new businesses with qualified personnel in the years to come. And in a general sense the country is indeed much more entrepreneurial than it used to be.

Filipe Carvalho is a self-made man, in Europe and not in Silicon Valley. To get there, he has paid a price. Yet his burden seems to have been light, he loves what he does. He is part of the growing group of Portuguese rebuilding their country's economy, bridging the gap between high-tech and existing services. Along the way he contributes to making the world a bit greener. And he is still married to his co-founder and wife, Ana. I imagine she must be smiling as she reads this – together they are beacons for young Europeans. Their persistence is definitely paying off.

FACTS ABOUT FILIPE CARVALHO:

NAME: Filipe Carvalho, Founder & CEO of Wide Scope
CIVIL STATUS: Married to Ana Pereira, co-founder of Wide Scope. They have two kids together.
BORN: 1977
FROM: Lisbon, Portugal

There is more to life than applying for poorly paid jobs with existing companies or the state.

EDUCATIONAL BACKGROUND: Master's degree in Mathematics from the University of Lisbon

What would you do if you were Prime Minister: I would definitely be fighting corruption as the hottest topic today.
What is the best thing about being a Portuguese entrepreneur: It is that we have a lot of opportunities to create something new in Portugal.
What is the worst thing about being a Portuguese entrepreneur: When you go abroad it sometimes feels like the Portuguese brand is a heavy weight to carry.

Three golden tips for young entrepreneurs:
1. Establish a good strategy.
2. Don't be whiny or complaining. The difficulties are there for everybody. Just hit the road and stop complaining!
3. Don't take it for granted that you will succeed. It takes longer than you believe, and success might not come for everyone.

THE PROTOTYPE FACTORY
Oslo

In Oslo, more and more prototype-workshops are opening. This is the future of business: The client is far more involved in product development than ever before.

In a modern building near The Hague's central railway station we find the TNO's offices. This is the Netherlands' business research institution. In order to get here visitors don't go through The Hague's picturesque city centre. The watchword here is efficiency. From our arrival at the railway station, it takes less than five minutes before we're in the reception. Shortly thereafter, we're in a meeting room. Across from us is professor Egbert-Jan Sol. He is the director of the programme "Smart Industry", as the Dutch have chosen to name the fourth industrial revolution.

Sol is happy to talk about what will happen in the future – but his focus is not flying cars or Virtual Reality (VR).

The purpose of Smart Industry is to give Dutch industry a competitive edge by rapidly integrating the possibilities that come from digitisation. This is what the aforementioned Wide Scope are doing. In addition, automated production systems and communicating robots will change industry as we know it. And a strong and innovative industry generates growth and jobs.

"Initially, the whole production structure will be completely automated. This isn't a trend, its happening."

Moreover, Sol explains that the future will consist of highly demanding consumers who might order anything at any time. This means that products have to be tailored to customers better than they are today. In the future, we won't be satisfied just ordering a couch. We may want to design parts of it ourselves, and this isn't limited to sofas: our cars and kitchen fittings will be custom designed. And that entails a change in logistics.

"I think you'll see more production and information sharing in the supply chain. If a business is going to produce individual parts while retaining mass production advantages, it has to automate, while at the same time a *block chain* is used to decentralise production."

Block chain is a technology wherein all product information is stored with all users, and updated every time anyone makes a change. The advantage of this technology is that it is difficult to hack, as alterations are quickly discovered. This is the same technology employed by the Estonian X-Road programme.

In the long-term, Sol also envisions stronger growth within 3D printing. At that point we may prefer to download and produce products at workshops close to where we live. He likens this to the media industry. We no longer buy films, books or records – we download content.

For European countries, this offers a number of challenges Sol says. In Germany, Industry 4.0 is about automation and customisation. That uniquely coloured car with a custom-made engine and select extras has to be available for order on a Monday and ready for pick-up Thursday afternoon. This means that the car has to be assembled on the production line as it's being ordered. Sol asks if we can imagine what the German automotive industry's nightmare is.

"It's that people can download the platform for a BMW or Mercedes and build it themselves. Of course the Germans also have another hurdle ahead, in that young people are buying fewer cars. They prefer hiring, borrowing or sharing."

In the Netherlands the situation is slightly different. They don't produce aircraft, weapons or cars, but small niche products. All the same, Sol imagines a future were products aren't necessarily produced by a producer, but en route to the customer. Manufacturers will make their money on leasing and updates, not on outright sales. Which means that money won't change hands in a single day, but over the course of years.

One consequence of this is that manufacturers won't need production facilities.

"Think of what's happened in the taxi and hotel industries. Booking agencies and taxi companies don't own property or cars anymore. Some regions in Europe will specialise, and there will be a lot of companies that don't manage the transition."

The reason why enormous amounts of money are required in industrial entrepreneurship is that both a prototype and a customer are needed to get things started, professor Sol explains. To develop a prototype that satisfies customer needs, you need money. Sol's viewpoint aligns with that of German entrepreneur Gleb Tritus, only on a much larger scale.

"The business needs to get to market. It's in conversations with the customer that you find out what works."

In this Sol feels that the Netherlands suffers from a cultural issue.

"We still want to develop the optimal solution before we start selling. But we can't manage that alone. We have to sell in order to find the optimal solution. That's why we're focussed on our students testing their concepts in the real world. Only when an idea has been tested do we believe it can work."

DREAMING OF A "CHEAP" PROTOTYPE

Abelia is the Confederation of Norwegian Enterprises' division for knowledge-based businesses. Currently Norway lacks experience when it comes to scaling up these types of enterprises.

"We have to remember that a lot of people in the business world today haven't previously started

This page is sponsored by www.morembo.no

companies. That means we have a lack of experience in what it means to be an entrepreneur and building businesses into large-scale companies."

He draws a parallel to the oil sector, which is currently heavily downsizing.

"You can find some expertise in the oil business and transfer it to other sectors, but some of the knowledge is industry-specific. You can't necessarily do med-tech or life-science if you've been in petroleum all your life."

Switching industries is one thing, creating a company is something entirely different. According to Ras-Vidal, the transition from being an employee to running your own business is extremely wide. All of a sudden you have to file VAT-returns, keep accounts, get your own coffee, and don't think your work will just sell itself. It is in order to ease that transition somewhat that Norway needs to build-up new ecosystems.

"If we exclude the fish-industry, oil, and shipping, where we already have good ecosystems in place, there aren't that many people who've done this before."

Today, we need arenas that can get new products to market fast.

"You have to focus on clients early. There are, of course, areas where this can be difficult, for example in "life sciences", but even there I feel that it's important to see one's first investor as a client."

He feels the investor is buying a lottery ticket, which means that he or she believes in the project. Either way, positive cash flow is important which means the prototype has to hit the market fast. His vision is to make advanced technology available for companies that cannot afford it today.

"I think we have to invest properly in expanding open laboratories where companies can have their prototypes built. These could be in science parks or otherwise clustered together. We think it's a good idea to have these laboratories in the same place. The idea is that the more people this benefits, the better it will be. It's a heavy investment for the business community, and so specializing a bit might be a good idea. In Bergen, for example, it might be obvious to focus on ocean technologies," says Ras-Vidal.

Fredrik Winther at Oslo Innovation Week agrees. And in his opinion, this is already happening to a certain degree.

"There are several "maker spaces" being made in Oslo right now. Examples of such are Bitraf and "Fellesverkstedet". Some of them are tied to schools and universities, and most are directed towards what we might call digital crafts. Potentially, they could make prototypes or handle small-scale production of physical objects."

To date, this has been very expensive. Often, sending one's plans to China has been the only viable alternative.

"Today, there is a huge potential for mid-range businesses (SMBs) that produce objects that will contain advanced technology."

This page is sponsored by Tor Erling Fagermoen, Oslo

"Industrialization is about implementing products. That's why we try to improve the procurement system, and try to bring down the price of innovation."

THE SHARED WORKSHOP

I'm standing in front of an old warehouse in what is not exactly Oslo's finest neighbourhood. I knock on the door, and Graham Hayward opens. He apologizes for not opening the door instantaneously.

"On Monday and Tuesday we had a load of architect-students come in. They were learning how to make models of houses with a 3D printer. Today is more calm."

As I step inside, the first thing I see is a giant crane. Not to mention a factory. Large parts of the room are covered in plastic.

"It's hard to stay warm here when it's 18 below outside. So, we made a tent around the digital lab and the printing press, so that it wouldn't be so cold to work there," Graham explains.

Graham is the founder of "Fellesverkstedet" (a shared workshop). He explains that initially Fellesverkstedet's target customers were artists, with a grass-roots approach.

"I realized that artists in Oslo lacked production facilities for large-scale works of art. And that getting high quality printing done was difficult. All while the number of studios in Oslo was decreasing."

Hence his goal was to set up a workshop where artists could come to work and at the same time assemble large pieces for exhibitions in Oslo.

"A key premise is that "we", being Fellesverkstedet, don't produce anything. We put the space and the

This page is sponsored by Sparebanken Vest, Bergen

production equipment at artists' disposal so that they can produce things themselves."

It was while creating this production space that Graham came to the realization that artists weren't the only ones in need of this type of facility. It was the entire creative sector, including architects, designers, and craftsmen. Around that time the designer Jens Dyvik came on board.

"I had done my personal research project, where I travelled around the world studying "FabLabs" – in other words, shared spaces where people have access to technology that lets them do their own production."

The force that drives FabLabs is that good, proven production techniques are becoming available as their patents expire. Thus, 3D printers are becoming available to a lot of people.

"I wanted to find out how a designer could make a living sharing technology. When I came home, I had made up my mind to start a FabLab."

He discovered that Fellesverkstedet had the same ideas in mind, which made cooperation the only sensible thing to do.

TECHNOLOGY AND KNOW-HOW FOR THE MASSES

Now Fellesverkstedet has built-up a sizeable technology park. They have large saws, laser-cutters, 3D printers, a printing press and a robot arm. Users pay a daily rate, and Fellesverkstedet puts the technology at their disposal, along with advice on how the tools can be used.

In many ways they are themselves a sort of prototype of what Sol was describing.

"What do you do if an entrepreneur shows up with a good idea, for example for building a drone?"

"First, we ask what experience that person has. Does he or she have a draft or not? Then we have to find out what functionality the drone is meant to have, whether it's a prototype or some form of industrial type. Then whether she thought of the controls and what materials it should be made of. When that's all done, we show her how she can make it herself."

There is a lot of consultation.

"For every penny we spend on technology, we spend the same on wages due to consulting," says Graham.

The users, on the other hand, have to invest their own working hours.

"We give people access to technology. Technology previously used in weapons and aircraft production. The people who worked there, thought inside their boxes. But when that tech is made available to people from a completely different background, new ideas take shape."

He calls it the difference between curated and un-curated structure.

"If you go to Innovation Norway (the government's national development bank), they'll choose the projects that they believe in. If you go to an incubator, you're curated along the same lines. The same thing goes with

This page is sponsored by Sverre Holm, Oslo

startup academies. At Fellesverkstedet, you can test your own idea."

This forces the user to experiment with the technology. They learn how something works, but also how the same technology might not work.

"You learn from your mistakes. It's rare that you get that experience in a school. There you're told that some things work and some don't. That makes it extremely difficult to make something no-one has thought of before."

And it's this mix of classic craftsmanship, technology, and letting users do things on their own, that Graham and Jens feel make Fellesverkstedet globally unique.

SMALL AND MEDIUM-SIZED BUSINESSES (SMB'S)

This structure makes it possible for an entrepreneur to make cheap prototypes. This makes it possible to get the product to market quickly. And an entrepreneur with technical skills as well as a good idea will control the entire production process.

"We had a violin maker who wanted to create an education program for music. After he had landed a deal with the philharmonic, he came in and made 150 mini-violins. Another industrious maker is Henning Pedersen. He runs a company called makeadrone.net, and produces his own kits for building drones."

The entire setup makes it possible for entrepreneurs to compete with big players.

"I mentioned that we'd had a visit from some students of architecture. They learn 3D modelling during the course of their programme, which means they can start working while they're still studying. As a result, they can participate in competition with other companies, like the renowned architectural firm "Snøhetta". Previously, you couldn't have done that, since you could not afford the technology."

Not all companies using the space become large employers, but that doesn't bother Dyvik.

"We won't have a lot of businesses with 5000 employees in the future. What we need are people who can create their own jobs. It's about a psychological change. And we think employers will need people who have technical skills and the ability to produce good things. Here, we can help you create, and you get to try your project out right away."

Maybe one of these companies will become a colossus in the future?

MEDICAL TECHNOLOGY

The big question for Norway is, in which sectors can industries be built? One sector that isn't numerically very big, but which nevertheless represents an important cluster of enterprises, is the education sector. In recent years, Norwegian companies like "Kahoot", "We want to know", and "Crecora" have been established.

However, if we look at potential turnover, the health sector presents greater possibilities. "Oslo

This page is sponsored by Lars Monrad-Krohn, Oslo

Medtech" is a cluster of enterprises that has grown quite rapidly. Fredrik Winther feels that a comparative advantage for Norway may lie in the country's large public health service, which represents a correspondingly large consumer of services.

"There are pros and cons to it. The downside is that it's really difficult to get into the frame as a bidder in the Norwegian health service. But on the upside, there's a big market, which bears experimenting."

As Winther thinks this over, he grows enthusiastic. Imagine if one thousandth of the health budget went towards innovation?

One thousandth of the health budget is more than all other purchases in the innovation game combined.

"Everyone is entitled to health care. So it's an obvious growth industry," says Kathrine Myhre.

Oslo Medtech is a cluster of health technology enterprises whose aim is to accelerate and support the development of new medical technology and e-health products as well as services for the Norwegian and global health market.

Currently the cluster has around 190 members, and the whole production chain is represented, adds Myhre, who is the general manager.

The cluster's goal is to create an industry of sustainable health technology and services that ensure quality treatment.

Medtech intends to achieve this by creating growth in existing enterprises and establishing new businesses.

That's why they are establishing an incubator for their industry in the capital. In short, it's about industrializing world-class technologies.

"Industrialization is about implementing products. That's why we try to improve the procurement system, and try to bring down the price of innovation."

The price of innovation must fall if Western countries are not to buckle under the weight of their elderly citizens. She gives an example:

"The company HY5 develops – using 3D printing, advanced composites, and robotics – a prosthetic hand with extremely high functionality. Thanks to the reasonable production that 3D printing allows, it can be offered at a very cost-effective price."

Nevertheless, it is important to evaluate whether Oslo Medtech is actually supporting growth in the industry.

"When we started, there were no statistics for the medical technology sector. We have to have metrics if we're going to measure the sector's potential for growth."

Myhre tells me that in 2013, their members had gross revenues of 37 billion kroner. That was a rise of 5.7 per cent from 2012. In Boston, growth was "only" 4.9 per cent. She is proud to say that 25 per cent of member companies derive 80 per cent of their revenue from international clients.

The point of a cluster is that you can scale-up through cooperation, Myhre points out. Cooperation

This page is sponsored by Anna Erlandsen, Oslo

can be in the form of creating a shared laboratory or shared testing.

This is precisely the type of laboratory that Ras-Vidal from Abelia has envisioned. And again, the point is to build cheaper prototypes. Myhre says that getting hospitals to take part in the process is crucial.

"By working with hospitals, we can do clinical trials of the technology. At the same time, we're working to get big companies to notice the Norwegian potential – we're trying to get Siemens to build their testing lab in Oslo."

She tells me about a joint project Oslo Medtech has with the intervention centre at Oslo University Hospital. It was actually a clinic where surgeons could practice using new technology. Once upon a time, the intervention centre staff managed to perform closed-chest cardiac surgery. The idea is that entry is made through the groin, using camera-bearing instruments, and the entire operation is controlled from a screen, as opposed to open surgery, where the patient's chest cavity is opened.

"Since Oslo Medtech didn't have any test facilities or its own laboratory, we asked the intervention centre if a few businesses could offer their technology to be tested by the centre's staff. And now they can. It's vital for the startups, while at the same time, surgeons really get to test new tech and aren't left with outdated knowledge."

"One company that proved their technology this way was "Conseptomed", who have developed a syringe that may be controlled using only one hand."

If a technology works, the business can quickly bring it to market. "Conseptomed" has already found millions in investments to start production.

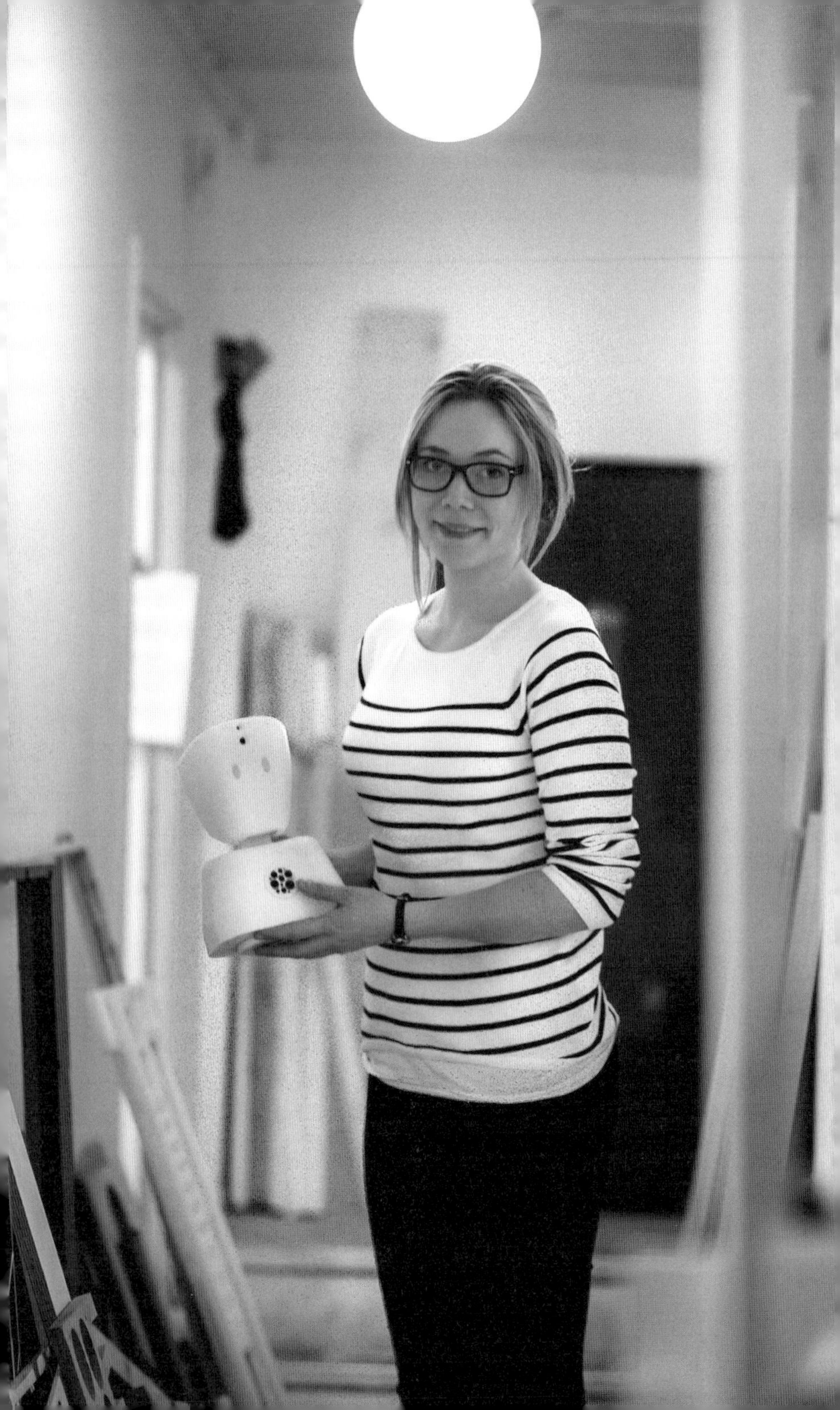

In under a year Karen Dolva has gone from concept to production of her avatar robot. While the avatar brings children with long-term illness back into the classroom, she uses her skills to bring in the necessary seed money to make large-scale production possible.

ENTREPRENEUR 3

THE LIVING AVATAR

Oslo

The idea for an avatar came in the summer of 2015. It would be controlled by, as well as functioning as the eyes, mouth and ears of a sick child. The robot's eyes and ears capture what the pupil needs to see and hear to participate virtually in lessons, while the remote pupil can talk back to the class through the robot's speaker. This alleviates one of the worst aspects of illness, isolation.

The Oslo-born Karen Dolva, seemingly without any inhibitions, is gifted with two great entrepreneurial qualities: Optimism and the ability to work hard. As she is at least as good a spokesperson as her robot, her newly established company "No Isolation" has already found large sums of seed money from angel investors.

For if the avatar is to hit mass production by summer 2016, as she plans, there's no time to waste.

Way up in a cramped loft at the makerspace "Bitraf" at Youngstorget in Oslo, traditionally known as the heart of the labour movement, sits a talkative interaction designer, a nearly finished avatar, five other co-workers, and me. We're sitting in a worn, 90s leather sofa where Karen explains why she calls herself the "chatterbox". It's her job to inspire and convince outside investors, the media and not least, customers.

The core of "No Isolation", besides Karen, also comprises Marius Aabel, nicknamed the "encyclopaedia". He is the product developer who, according to Karen, "knows everything that needs to be known". Such a team is a pretty decent foundation on which to start a business.

"Marius Aabel and I began talking about starting something together the first time we met, four years ago," says Karen.

Their entry into entrepreneurship has been a little unorthodox – they really wanted to help someone, but who should it be?

"Two years ago I thought about making a communications solution for the elderly. At that time, we really didn't really hit on anything. We could neither define the bigger issue nor envision the big fix. So, we went our separate ways again."

During the summer of 2015 something happened, Karen became acquainted with a lady by the name of Anne Fi Troje. Troje had lost her daughter to cancer some years earlier after a long drawn-out period of illness.

ISOLATION IS THE WORST FOR SICK KIDS

"She told me that the isolation was the worst thing for her daughter, not the rough treatment or the way the disease progressed. It knocked me completely out. All of a sudden, we had a much more engaging problem, one we could sacrifice everything for!"

Marius quit his job only two days after Karen's conversation with Anne Troje, eager to create a solution for this group of children.

"We were fairly certain that as long as we found a real problem, we'd be able to solve it. It was far more important finding what we wanted to work and be passionate about, than finding the specific product," explains Karen.

That was the summer of 2015. Then, for three months, she waited for Marius to finish his contract with his former employer. However, Karen did not waste the time. During these three months, the avatar's requirements were mapped out. Karen worked on finding a tool that could connect the long-term sick children with their friends and teachers. Not primarily to avoid lost progression at school, but to avoid disconnection from day-to-day fellowship.

"I had to find out what the kids' needs were. What did they miss, being away from their friends and school for such a long time?"

There was nothing to do but to get down to it and interview as many of them as possible, as well as to talk to teachers and parents to find out where their actual problems lay. Thus the image of the avatar emerged, little by little.

"It wasn't until October 2015 that we knew what we'd be making. Now, a little over three months later, we have our prototype ready. It's gone as quickly as we said it would. We promised to have it ready by the middle of December 2015 – and we did," says Karen.

She can't praise her team enough. For more people in addition to Marius were soon to join. In only six months, Karen and her team have created a talking avatar. It may be an incarnation of the entrepreneur herself, who in the course of those six months has brought in two rounds of seed investors.

The summer of 2016, "No Isolation's" robot starts manual production in Oslo. That is exciting in and of itself, after decades where most Norwegian industrial production has been discontinued and outsourced to China. Their goal is to have robots ready for delivery as schools start in the autumn of 2016.

The avatars will be rented out to parents of children with long-term illnesses. The idea is to see positive financial results as soon as possible. The Nordic market is the first step, which will be conquered simultaneously

This page is sponsored by www.morembo.no

with the Norwegian market. After that, she wants to expand into the UK, the Netherlands as well as the USA. She believes her avatar can go far.

THE UNEXPECTED INVESTORS

Today, No Isolation has ten employees. Keeping such a group up and running takes money. Marius Aabel has turned 40, and has an apartment and a life he would like to continue. He was quick to let Dolva know that he wouldn't work hand-to-mouth, as the much younger Karen was prepared to do for a while. That kind of existence wouldn't give him any energy to concentrate.

His firm demands have actually been positive for them. That made it clear that investments would be needed for "No Isolation" to succeed. As the saying goes, money doesn't grow on trees, but must be gathered, investor-by-investor. And that is where "the chatterbox" comes into her own.

"In the first round, we found NOK5 million [just under £500,000] from angel investors. Neither of us had any kind of money to throw in, but we invest an awful lot of hours. Now, we also pay ourselves a little. Effectively, that means we have enough not to live on the street, that we eat OK, and that we can afford electricity and Internet at home," Karen explains.

Leaving aside her cohort's age and experience, Karen herself has been well schooled, three years at the incubator "StartupLab" in Oslo. There, she saw that startups that planned a growth strategy for their company

"It is important to treat everyone you meet as a potential investor. Chasing the big names is not always what is important."

often succeeded. The ones who just talked about their product, on the other hand, were often left banging their heads against the wall. She also became acquainted with the large investment scene surrounding the incubator, but found that it wasn't necessarily the most professional among them who would be her most important investors.

"I got in touch with those I thought might be interested. We got a few polite "thanks, but no, thanks" but also a few surprising thumb up. As it turns out people I never envisaged as angel investors have become precisely that. If you meet the right people at the right time," Karen points out, "people you never thought would be on your side can turn out to be your most dedicated supporters."

"It is important to treat everyone you meet as a potential investor. Chasing the big names is not always what is important."

The team is now getting positive feedback. People understand that they're trying to solve an actual problem, and thereby satisfy a market need. Almost half the angels investing in this project are women who are familiar with or understand the problem. They aren't just investing financially, but in a solution to a problem that many find very challenging.

"Now, we're in the process of finding two to three million dollars of seed funding. This is all new for us. The learning curve is sometimes scarily steep.

Now Karen and her team also know who has the right kind of money.

"We've been very fortunate to find a co-owner in Martin Hauge, who was a partner at Creandum. He also founded Creuna and a number of other companies before that. He knows the game."

NO SUPPORT FROM MOTHER

According to Statistics Norway (SSB), only 30 per cent of Norwegian entrepreneurs are women. How did Karen start her own company?

"If my mother had her choice, I'd be working in a bank! I would have studied at the Norwegian School of Economics in Bergen, but luckily, I didn't have time to enrol there before I started studying interaction design at the University of Oslo."

Since she was young Karen has liked playing with ideas and bringing projects to life. However it wasn't until her years at StartupLab in Oslo that she quite grasped what it would take to start a commercially viable business. Previously she thought offering a good product would be enough. Gradually she learned that this wasn't the case. It was those with the will to grow who found success. They also had a clear plan to work from, even if it had to be revised along the way.

KNOW WHAT YOU WANT

Her colleague Marius leans into the conversation. He tells me that life-style entrepreneurs are burgeoning at

This page is sponsored by www.morembo.no

the moment. That is people who want the lifestyle, the freedom and chance to think creatively, but not the actual work of bringing their ideas to life. He was probably in that category himself at first, but quickly understood that there was a lot of work involved. That makes having a goal all the more important.

"Nobody works this much if they don't know what they really want. Contributing to solving a need for a big group of people around the world is meaningful. It makes the hours worth it," he says.

"I have two much younger siblings. When Anne Fi Troje told us about her teenage daughter, it struck straight home. My reaction was, "Of course, this has to be solved!""

Karen Dolva has always loved to communicate.

"Every job I've done has dealt with communication. This group of children with long-term illnesses is isolated. I asked myself, "What communication-tools already exist for them?" I saw that this field had developed slowly. That's when I found the crux. This was where I found a problem that matched well both my own abilities and motivation."

Marius continues, "Ever since I was a little boy, I've made new things. Making something and having everyone around me use it is my biggest joy. From around 17, I was constantly making software-based stuff. I sold programs and software."

Yet, he dreamt of making something physical.

"It's completely amazing. When you're doing it, it's hard to go to sleep at night, to put it like that!" The product developer becomes starry-eyed, and it becomes clear why he is exactly that, a product developer.

But of course, it takes more than two to tango in this game. Here after all, an almost living avatar will be created.

"I think that when you're building a team that's going to manage something this crazy with so few resources, there has to be some personality overlap in the group so people understand one another. At the same time, the team has to cover the entire spectrum of things needing to be done. It's not just about building the robot. It's equally important to find customers, investors, and maintain a relationship to the public," he explains.

Karen points out how since day one, customer interaction has been important. They are the ones who have the need. That has been a constant focus for the team. She doesn't dwell too much on the fear of failure.

"I feel a lot of people talk about rough patches and adversity. But, if I think of it as two weeks ago, I didn't know what I know today, I can't see that as failure. It's much easier being an entrepreneur, then. Everyone says they hit a wall. But we haven't hit any walls, though we have had a lot of "no's" along the way!"

Should "No Isolation" not succeed in the way Karen is thinking and hoping it will, that's OK too. She is content today, and will be so tomorrow.

This page is sponsored by www.morembo.no

"I think that when you're building a team that's going to manage something this crazy, there has to be some personality overlap in the group so people understand one another."

There is a stiff breeze sweeping Youngstorget this Friday afternoon. For Karen, Marius, and the rest of the group at "No Isolation", it's mostly been a warm and favourable wind so far. Still, it's looking forward that matters. When the planned avatars are delivered in August, they have to be able to show solid sales figures from the start. Logistics and support-functions will also have to be in place.

The Oslo "chatterbox" will be doing her bit to make all this reality in due time. Sometimes, that's the most important thing, talking a good game.

FACTS ABOUT KAREN DOLVA

DATE OF BIRTH: 18/5/1990
PLACE OF BIRTH: Oslo
EDUCATION: Interaction Design, Institute of Computer Science, University of Oslo

What would you do if you were Prime Minister for a day? I'd do away with the wealth tax, at least for working capital. Then, I'd do away with all types of support schemes from the government, and rather issue a guaranteed minimum income instead. It won't be long before technology drastically reduces the need for labour. I think we have to change our idea of working. I have also been fooled into believing that an inheritance tax is a good idea. It would be interesting if everyone had the same starting point. Luckily, I am not the Prime Minister!

This page is sponsored by www.inclusion.no

What is the best thing about being a Norwegian entrepreneur? The best thing is that there is a home market in Norway where it's easy to try out new technology. On top of which, we have really secure safety nets in the welfare state, should we as entrepreneurs fall down utterly. Wages for good programmers are far more reasonable here than in the US!

What is the worst thing about being an entrepreneur in Norway? The tax code. In Norway, there aren't any good incentives to invest. And the wealth tax is a pain for those of us starting companies. Add to which, we're used as circus acrobats. Right now, entrepreneurs are the "in thing", which means we have to be up for anything.

THREE GOLDEN TIPS FOR YOUNG ENTREPRENEURS:

1. Find the right people to start your business with. Find a mentor who has done this "a million times" before.
2. Have a plan with milestones. Don't be afraid to change the details, but be aware before you change a milestone.
3. Don't worry if you don't know the field you're getting into. You'll learn it, anyway – you'll find out things when you need to!
4. Everyone says not to be afraid of failure. I think we're just as scared to succeed here in the North.

What will we do if we make it…? I completely panic at the idea, so don't be afraid of success.
5. Don't partake in too much fun and games. Startup competitions don't reflect the real world, so make sure that a competition will be good for your company.

PART 2: From concept to industrial growth?

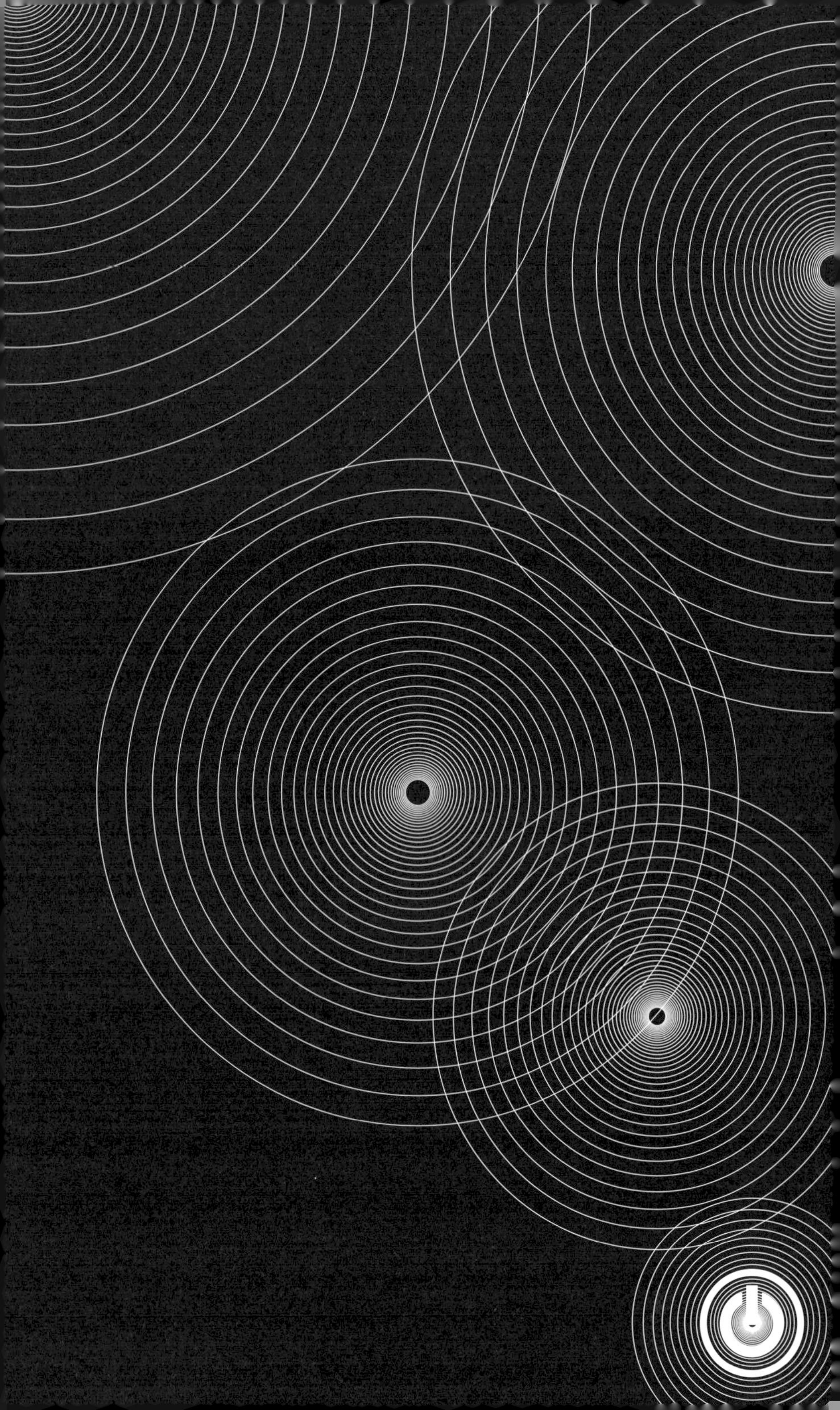

Part 3: WORK FOR ALL

Europe's challenge is to create enough jobs. When the entrepreneurial spirit flows through all sectors, the economy grows and new jobs are created.

In 1972 the unemployment rate in West Germany rose above two per cent for the first time since 1950. Although no one realized it at the time, this signalled the end of an era. By the 1970s the impact of industry on total European GDP had started its decline.

The industrial revolution had brought about a demand for unskilled labour that lasted over a hundred years. A 16 year old born in 1950 could go to sea, find work in a coalmine, or undergo a quick apprenticeship and become a steel worker. In those days a steel worker had to be strong and tough. At the time coal and had to be shovelled into furnaces by hand at a gruelling pace. It was time-consuming and took a lot of manpower. By the 1970s pure brawn wasn't enough anymore. Automation started and suddenly one only needed to press a button to dump four tonnes of lime into the furnace. Now, skilled labour was needed to run the machines.

This doesn't mean that there are no industries that need unskilled labour. The retail industry and the service sector do, but not everyone can make their living pulling pints for each other. So the market for unskilled labour is limited. A consequence of the big shifts of the 1970s was that large industrial centres like Manchester, Dortmund, and Turin started losing residents. Large segments of the population became passive.

We are living in the middle of the fourth industrial revolution, which will be characterized by the digitization of services and automation. In the 1970s it was unskilled labourers who lost their jobs in the mines and on the production line. Today the retail industry is feeling the pressure from online shopping, accountants and clerks have to compete with digital services, and no one knows quite what will happen to the transport industry if self-driving cars become the norm.

Since the 70s northern Europe has met this challenged with a firm belief in higher education. It is a logical response, encourage young people to study their way out of unemployment. But it doesn't help people who drop out of high school. How do we find jobs for those who aren't highly educated?

THE PROBLEM OF INCLUSION

Finding enough jobs for people without higher education is also an answer to a potential integration issue, something which can be seen in Sweden. Sweden has the lowest level of employment among its migrant population in Europe. This is often seen as a cause of radicalization, as is consistently pointed out in France and Belgium. And the problem of integration can also be seen in Estonia. Rainer Kattel explains that in Estonia there is a young male elite who basically only think about innovation and economic growth.

"The elite want to make Estonia wealthy. Conversely, they haven't concerned themselves with social problems."

This has led to a rising problem with poverty-stricken Russians, who are one of the country's minorities.

This page is sponsored by Olugboyega Olusoga, London

According to Kattel, Russian-speakers were unable to handle the transition from Soviet to market economy.

"They were successful in industry until 1991, but it's closed down now. There are only a few minority representatives left as their voices in parliament." This is reflected in the average life expectancy for Estonian men, largely minority males, being very low.

In Estonia, frustrated Russians are easy prey for Vladimir Putin's Russian nationalism. The cohesion of Estonian society is at stake. As Europe accepts more and more refugees, the economy's ability to create jobs will be decisive.

Regardless of whom we ask, we are told a variation on the same theme. Europe has to create a business climate where entrepreneurs can scale up their businesses, and the startup spirit found in the IT-sector has to spread to other sectors. We have to create a stronger service economy. Perhaps the cycle delivery service Foodora and Uber can provide a way into the job market. One country that managed to stimulate economic growth in several sectors (prior to Brexit) is the UK.

THE MIRACLE OF JOBS

The first thing I see as I exit the Underground at Old Street is a colossal television screen. Bang in the middle of a roundabout the world's leading IT-company, Google, has created a mix between a billboard and 24-hour news channel. Assorted Google products slide across the screen: A map, a weather forecast and a stream of headlines. The calendar tells me it's May. A second poll of the day has David Cameron's Tories and Ed Miliband's Labour in a dead heat. I've come to Hackney and the Old Street roundabout to peer into the future.

Old Street is at the heart of Hackney. Strictly speaking of course I'm in Shoreditch, which is part of Hackney, which in turn is the area of London with the most startups. London has the most startups in the UK. And the UK has the most startups in Europe. According to National Statistics, 1.3 million jobs have been created in the UK since 2010. A stunning 40 per cent of those jobs have been created by businesses started less than five years ago.

This has led to British unemployment dropping from eight per cent in May 2010 to about five per cent in April 2016. Although the UK has, historically speaking, had lower unemployment than the European average, these are impressive figures all the same. Only since early 2014, the number of unemployed has gone down by 1.8 per cent. By comparison Eurozone unemployment is at 10.3 per cent and Britain's old nemesis, France, has 10.5 per cent of its labour force out of work.

In the last few years Hackney has been dubbed "Tech City" by the media, owing to all the tech and design startups that have taken root in the old working class area. And they're aiming for the stars every day – Hackney is "a dream come true" for the educated middle class. A vibrant creative industry has become a

This page is sponsored by Gary Klopfenstein, Chicago

reality, and Hackney is now where trend and lifestyle editors for the Saturday papers come in search of inspiration.

On the right hand side of Old Street, I have a view of all the skyscrapers between London and Tower Bridge. In their midst towers "The Shard", the tallest building in Europe. On the 17th floor, Professor Mark Hart is giving me a private lecture about the UK's entrepreneurship boom.

Hart manages the Global Entrepreneurship Monitor (GEM) UK team, a part of the GEM Global research project, and he is also Deputy Director of the National Enterprise Research Centre (ERC). ERC's mandate is to explore the question: "What drives growth in small and medium-sized businesses?" He also advises the UK government on entrepreneurship policy based on his experience working with small and medium-sized businesses through Goldman Sachs' *10,000 Small Businesses* program, which he leads for the Midlands region of the UK.

"Britain has uncoupled itself from the rest of the continent in the entrepreneurship stakes. We definitely have the most entrepreneurial population in Europe, which is confirmed by recent OECD statistics. In terms of the number of companies started, we're right between the US and the rest of continental Europe."

In 2014, 8.5 per cent of the British working age population said that they would start their own businesses within the next three years.

"The interesting thing is that a full 25 per cent of the Britons who said they wanted to start their own business, actually did it. Only two per cent of the French followed through. I don't know why that's the case. Either the French and the British are interpreting the question differently, or the French are finding out that it's too hard," reflects Hart.

He thinks the main reason is that the UK has a more business-friendly environment than France.

"We tried to set up a new venture in France, but we gave up. No-one could tell us how to start a viable company there."

Hart explains that young people represent a significant proportion of the increased number of UK entrepreneurs. In fact, the number of young entrepreneurs has doubled since 2002. It seems like the UK has cracked the nut that is stymying Europe: How to foster entrepreneurship and combat harmful unemployment among young people.

HIGH SPIRITS IN OFFICE LANDSCAPES

It is therefore no wonder that spirits are high in London's many shared offices for startups. In Hackney, they're 13 to the dozen, and business hopefuls looking to find shared office space can find it at coworkinglondon.com. Big names are Trampery, Netil 360, and the Oval Office.

What makes Hackney hip however, is not its cool coworking spaces with their egg-shaped chairs and

This page is sponsored by Eyvind Olafsrud, Port Moresby

fancy coffee makers, it is lower property prices. The area is still one of the cheapest districts in London. The combination of big city and low prices is like fly paper to creative types, which is why so many artists and galleries first came here.

In the 1990s a group of artists and galleries packed their bags and moved to cheap old Hackney, last outpost of the artistic East End, which stretches from Whitechapel to Hoxton Square. Hoxton Square is also the location of the famed White Cube gallery, displaying British contemporary artists like Damien Hirst, Tracy Emin, and Dino Chapman.

The next few years saw a lot of champagne flow in Hackney as art collectors came pouring in. Hot on their heels came more creative institutions such as the London College of Fashion. Bars, clothes shops, and galleries popped up all over the place. Nightclubs and restaurants gave the area a cool reputation which drew in developers. So, now they're building – Old Street is surrounded by new high-rises. Two new high-rises have just been finished on City Street alone.

Hackney is booming, but it is not only Hackney's entrepreneurial scene that is driving Britain's economic growth.

"We're seeing growth in all sectors of the economy."

"Tech startups have no better chance of being successful than companies in any other sector. Retail, wholesale, and manufacture – which also contain many examples of high tech – are growing at least as fast as the tech companies," explains Hart.

Being an entrepreneur has a different vibe than before. Hart feels that the way entrepreneurs are depicted in popular culture shows how their image has changed.

"In TV-shows from the 60s, entrepreneurs were depicted as operating in low value-added activities such as "Steptoe and Son" - someone travelling around selling things he'd found – selling scrap, really. Then, in the 70s, the entrepreneur was again portrayed as someone shady, on the margins of legality. The ITV gave us businessmen like scheming Arthur Daley - a second hand car dealer. In the 1980s, the BBC gave us "Only Fools and Horses" which depicted the Trotter family as opportunistic and barely legal entrepreneurs."

"It wasn't until the 2000s that we got a slightly more realistic depiction of entrepreneurs on British television through for example the reality shows "*Dragons Den*" and "*The Apprentice*". The format in the former is that entrepreneurs present their business idea to four rich investors who give their feedback and, occasionally, financial support."

"The combination of these new TV shows and the vibe from Hackney have made entrepreneurship appear attractive, and politicians now benefit when talking about entrepreneurship empowering young people," says Sarah Fink.

Sarah Fink works for the think tank "Centre for Entrepreneurship" in London, which exists to bolster

This page is sponsored by Gary Klopfenstein, Chicago

the British public's entrepreneurial spirit. Their address is in Berkley Square, a legendary green oasis in the city centre and one of London's most exclusive addresses – where Winston Churchill grew up next door to Charles Rolls, who would go on to start his own business and produce a reasonably well-known line of cars.

"Entrepreneurship has become trendy," reaffirms Fink.

"It is partly down to the tech clusters in East London. They're selling this image that you can do what you want and live a flexible lifestyle. We don't know exactly how much the IT startups are making – a lot of them aren't making anything at all – but regardless, it's providing people with work, and creating new jobs for the British economy," she continues.

The interesting thing is that the entrepreneurial spirit is spreading from Hackney to other parts of the city.

"People are starting coworking spaces in other parts of London. For example, they've started a media hub in Bloomsbury, which is good. It's a lot better for people in the media to work near the existing media-companies in Bloomsbury than in slightly cheaper Hackney."

However Fink is unsure of how much what has worked in Hackney might apply to other countries.

"Hackney is booming right now because it's cheap. In established areas, gentrification happens when pressure from the housing market is strong enough."

Attitudes towards starting one's own business have also changed in British business.

"Businesses today accept that careers can be built on a multitude of platforms. Even if your business doesn't succeed, a prospective employer won't see you as a failure. That means the risk of starting a business is far smaller than one might think," says Dr Jeff Skinner.

Jeff Skinner is the executive director of "London Business School" and head of the business incubator "Deloitte Institute of Innovation and Entrepreneurship". He also feels that a stronger focus on entrepreneurship in schools has changed the vibe.

"More and more people are seeing entrepreneurship as a career path. And that makes being in business for yourself "normal", which creates a critical mass of people interested in innovation."

Hart points out that a gender gap is appearing in the UK population.

"If we look at the population as a whole – that is, not just the ones who say they want to be entrepreneurs or are running their own business – we see that fear of failure has dropped among men. At the same time, it's risen to a record high amongst women. 48 per cent of UK women say that fear of failure is their main reason for not starting their own business."

MILLIONS OF ANGELS

Let's forget about the people who don't want to start their own business. Entrepreneurial optimism is making

This page is sponsored by Gary Klopfenstein, Chicago

more people want to help others start on their own. When return on investment (ROI) for savings is poor, more people want to invest in new businesses – in other words they become business angels.

According to the NESTA-report "The Rise of future finance", The UK alternative finance market grew by 91 per cent from £492m in 2012 to £939m in 2013. In June 2015, the Financial Times wrote that cumulative lending to SMEs totalled £1.581bn in June 2015. Alternative financing and peer to peer investment in manufacturing, technology and wholesale is a trend the British government appreciates and wants to stimulate through such schemes as SEIS and EIS providing tax breaks to investors.

Hart feels that the number of business angels is strengthened through this active investment policy. The Enterprise Investment Scheme (EIS) was created to help smaller and unquoted businesses (with a maximum of 250 employees) find financing. Anyone investing in such a company can deduct 30 per cent of investment costs from their taxes, up to a maximum of one million pounds. If you invest £10,000 you pay £3,000 less in taxes that year. And if you hang on to your shares for at least three years, they'll be exempt from capital gains tax as well.

As if that wasn't enough, if you lose money on your investment you can write off the loss against your income.

The Seed Enterprise Investment Scheme (SEIS) is for those who want to take a bigger chance. Investors

"Businesses today accept that careers can be built on a multitude of platforms. Even if your business doesn't succeed, a prospective employer won't see you as a failure."

putting money into companies with a maximum of 25 employees and two million pounds in revenue can deduct 50 per cent of their investment against their taxes, although this scheme does give somewhat lower deductions on subsequent gains.

The research report "A Nation of Angels" by the ERC points out that nearly 90 per cent of all angels have invested through the SEIS or EIS schemes.

Additionally, a number of new financing services have popped up online, where individuals offer loans or investments to startups. "Seedrs" is one such service, a platform for buying shares in newly established businesses. While through the site "Funding Circle" individuals can lend money to entrepreneurs.

Seedrs guarantees that companies on their site adhere to UK securities law, and handle administration, documentation, and payment for investors and businesses. An investor may invest as much or as little as they would like in voting shares. An investment through the site qualifies for SEIS, and in some cases EIS.

"The combination of crowdfunding, SEIS, and EIS has made being an angel investor an attractive proposition," explains Hart. "The way angels work has changed."

Todays' angels are younger and more women are getting involved.

Fink, at the Centre for Entrepreneurship, thinks that the combination of websites like Seedrs and EIS and SEIS is changing the British economy.

"London is a world leader in crowdfunding, far ahead of New York and San Francisco. 79 per cent of angels take advantage of the tax relief, and 43 per cent made their investment through crowdfunding."

She stresses that this is also due to an increase in the number of younger angels.

"Today, 44 per cent of angels are below 45 years of age. And the number of female angels, 14 per cent, has doubled since 2008, and they are very active in crowdfunding."

Seedrs gives a relative advantage to British businesses. This type of financial service has been illegal in large parts of the EU, as providing loans (Funding Circle) or selling securities (Seedrs) requires banking regulation.

In fact, not only private individuals are using these services. The British government has chosen to channel 60 million pounds into small business loans through Funding Circle.

Jeff Skinner at London Business School believes that many startups receive substantial funding through precisely such websites.

"These sites make information on the startups available to a new audience."

CREATE YOUR OWN JOB

Most of those who receive investments from private individuals and qualify for SEIS or EIS are entrepreneurs creating jobs. The Global Entrepreneurship Monitor

This page is sponsored by Gary Klopfenstein, Chicago

research project is tracking the levels of entrepreneurial activity in over 70 countries including the UK.

"We are particularly interested in entrepreneurs who employ people. Since we have access to statistics on all registered business in the UK (for VAT and payroll and income taxes from HMRC (Her Majesty's Revenue and Customs), we're able to see how many people are working for startups," says Hart.

As companies that create jobs are the ones driving economic growth, research undertaken by the national Enterprise Research Centre (ERC) focuses on employer enterprises and does not measure sole proprietorships nor traded companies without employees. But the number of self-employed is large and it is at an all-time high in the UK. In 2014 alone around 250,000 job-creating companies were established in the UK, but Company House reports that a total of 587,000 companies were started.

"That tells us one thing, which is that we have a strong trend of people creating their own jobs," Hart explains.

Many are young, and it is precisely this development that Izzy Hatfield at the progressive think tank "Institute for Public Policy Research" has been studying.

"40 per cent of all new jobs in the UK are newly started businesses, but a lot of these jobs aren't permanent positions," Hatfield says.

In total, one in seven jobs in the UK are self-employed.

"First off, I have to say that self-employment can be a brilliant opportunity. People can make use of new and exciting technologies to sell services or work as a consultant wherever they like."

Examples of this are Airbnb, Uber, and Elance. Elance is a portal for companies looking for freelancers such as programmers, designers, and writers.

"The coalition government introduced the New Enterprise Allowance programme, which is meant to stimulate people outside the job market to start their own business," says Hatfield.

People receiving unemployment benefits can get a mentor to help them develop a business plan. If the plan is approved, the applicant is given help to launch and sell their product or service, as well as a grant for 26 weeks. She or he may also apply for a starter loan. Fink, at the Centre for Entrepreneurship, points out that a lot of people receiving benefits have entered this programme. Hatfield, on the other hand, is less optimistic.

"Starting a business is a challenging process and earnings can be low and irregular at the outset. For some people the New Enterprise Allowance helps them to get a business off the ground, but it isn't a suitable solution for every job seeker."

Hatfield isn't saying that it's bad that a lot of businesses fail.

"Stimulating employment through supporting entrepreneurship is only effective in the long-run if the opportunity is a choice, rather than a last resort."

She feels that a lot of startup owners are in a precarious position. They are examples of what the DIHK in Germany calls "entrepreneurs by necessity".

"They can be people who have lost their job because of the economic crisis, and so they start their own business. They make more than they would on benefits, but less money than before. That's what you'll find – for example – with IT-consultants now running their own little consulting company."

Self-employment can be precarious for people across the skill spectrum.

"They may be tech-entrepreneurs, but the New Enterprise Allowance is also available to recent graduates and people who can't find any other job. They might start working as cleaners, hairdressers, or taxi-drivers, living from hand-to-mouth, maybe with a little extra money from a bank loan. These aren't exactly ground-breaking startups."

Hatfield's point is underscored by many startups being very poor earners. Even in IT entrepreneurs make 25 per cent less than those working at established businesses.

"A great deal of those involved in newly established businesses make so little money that they don't pay taxes." Self-employed workers have tended to have a lower average income than regular employees, which may in part be because they are on average less productive.

NOT THAT DARK

The aforementioned poor wage growth had analysts at the Bank of England worried. How was the central bank to interpret the fact that unemployment was falling while tax revenue stayed the same? In the report "*Self-employment: what can we learn from recent developments?*" the bank wrote that the lack of tax revenue and the boom of self-employed were the result of a structural shift within the labour market. While there has been an increase in the number of low turnover businesses, only four per cent of those who were self-employed at the end of 2014 were looking for another job, while seven per cent of permanent employees were looking for other jobs. The report concluded that the increase in poorly paid self-employed could be the result of trends showing more people wanting to work less than before.

Hart at GEM sees a different reason for the lack of growth.

"Since 2009, we've seen that there are two groups in particular who start businesses. People under 30, and men over 50."

Often, young entrepreneurs won't make a lot of money, but as their choice to go into business for themselves is also motivated by greater pay over time, poor income growth could be temporary. But Hart finds the group of men over 50 as interesting.

"Entrepreneurs over 50 can also be divided into two categories. One consists of asset-rich older men starting what I call a lifestyle business perhaps as a result of taking early retirement."

This group is similar to many young entrepreneurs, they start a business to fulfil their dreams or start a new career. Money isn't important to them, and they often want low working hours.

"The other group is the recently unemployed or asset-poor. In that way, you might say that for those over 50, both affluence and poverty are motivations for starting a business."

THE ENGLISH DISEASE

Poor wage growth may also be down to lifestyle entrepreneurs being less motivated than hungry young entrepreneurs. Another interpretation is that British entrepreneurs might be starting businesses in less productive sectors. There are two stories one can tell about the British economy. The positive one is that the economy has been able to create more than 1.3 million jobs in the past four years. The negative one is that productivity isn't growing on the British Isles.

The Economist wrote an article entitled "Under the Bonnet", in which they examined the productivity growth in various sectors across England. They found massive growth in industrial productivity, strong growth in administrative services, but a sharp decline in finance and pharmaceuticals.

"The British economy growing is not the result of increasing productivity, but more jobs. We are less productive than we should be, and I think that is down to labour being cheap, while at the same time, living on benefits is harder than it was before. That means less productive workers are being forced into the labour market," explains Hatfield.

Fink agrees that not all businesses are high-tech, nor require high levels of education, but she disagrees with the idea that low-tech businesses cannot deliver economic growth.

"We just examined the 50 fastest growing businesses started by women in the UK. Our baseline was that turnover had to have reached a minimum of £100,000 and at the most five million pounds. Then we spent three years studying the results."

Their findings were presented in the report "*Shattering Stereotypes: Women in Entrepreneurship*."

'What we found was that a lot of women were starting professional services like accountancy, marketing, and legal services.

"So, sectors with growing productivity?"

"Yes, but there were also a lot of catering, cleaning, and café businesses on the list. Those aren't businesses with stellar growth, but tried and true business models. The point is that women were succeeding with new concepts," says Fink.

Jeff Skinner at London Business School fills in a bit of detail.

"Companies that grow quickly, from two to five million pounds, face huge leadership challenges. In Britain, that's where we fall down. We don't have a startup problem, but a growth and management problem"

"Everyone is doing something with technology nowadays. Fairly few of the businesses in our incubator are tech-businesses, but they're all digitalized. Although the majority of our businesses may be in the service industry, we also have fashion companies," says Skinner.

He calls it "Spotify"-ification. Everybody is looking for a platform that will allow him or her to deliver different services. The irony is that Spotify has contributed to declining productivity in the record industry.

While the picture of entrepreneurship may be of technology-based startups, there are other industries on Hatfield's mind.

"I've been comparing sectors in the UK with corresponding sectors in Germany, Belgium, and France. The British service industry is a lot less productive than the French, which means there is potential for growth in low-productivity sectors, which are not traditionally a focus of government policy."

"Do you think people might have been displaced from productive jobs into less productive entrepreneurship?"

"It's certainly possible, but this only makes up for a small contribution to the UK's productivity puzzle," Hatfield replies.

LACK OF SKILLED JOBS AND MANAGEMENT

Mark Hart fears it might boil down to management.

"British companies also have a problem in regards to management. Management often doesn't have the skills to scale up an operation or expand internationally."

He points to the fact that 80 per cent of all businesses are not in business after ten years.

The UK is the European leader in entrepreneurship. It is a place where unemployment is going down and where young people are finding work. And yet the British entrepreneurial boom has had the unintended side effects of reduced tax revenue and poor productivity growth for the business sector as a whole. So the question is, is there a remedy for this? As far as entrepreneurs are concerned, Hart is sure he has the answer.

"Companies that grow quickly, from two to five million pounds, face huge leadership challenges. In Britain, that's where we fall down. We don't have a start-up problem, but a growth and management problem," he concludes.

The investment in entrepreneurship in schools and universities, stimulation through tax incentives, and portrayals of hip, young entrepreneurs in the media have the British public dreaming of starting their own businesses. The next step, says Hart, is training kids and teens to be good leaders. In order for the entrepreneurial spirit to effect growth, he concludes, Britain must teach the entrepreneurs of tomorrow, good leadership skills today.

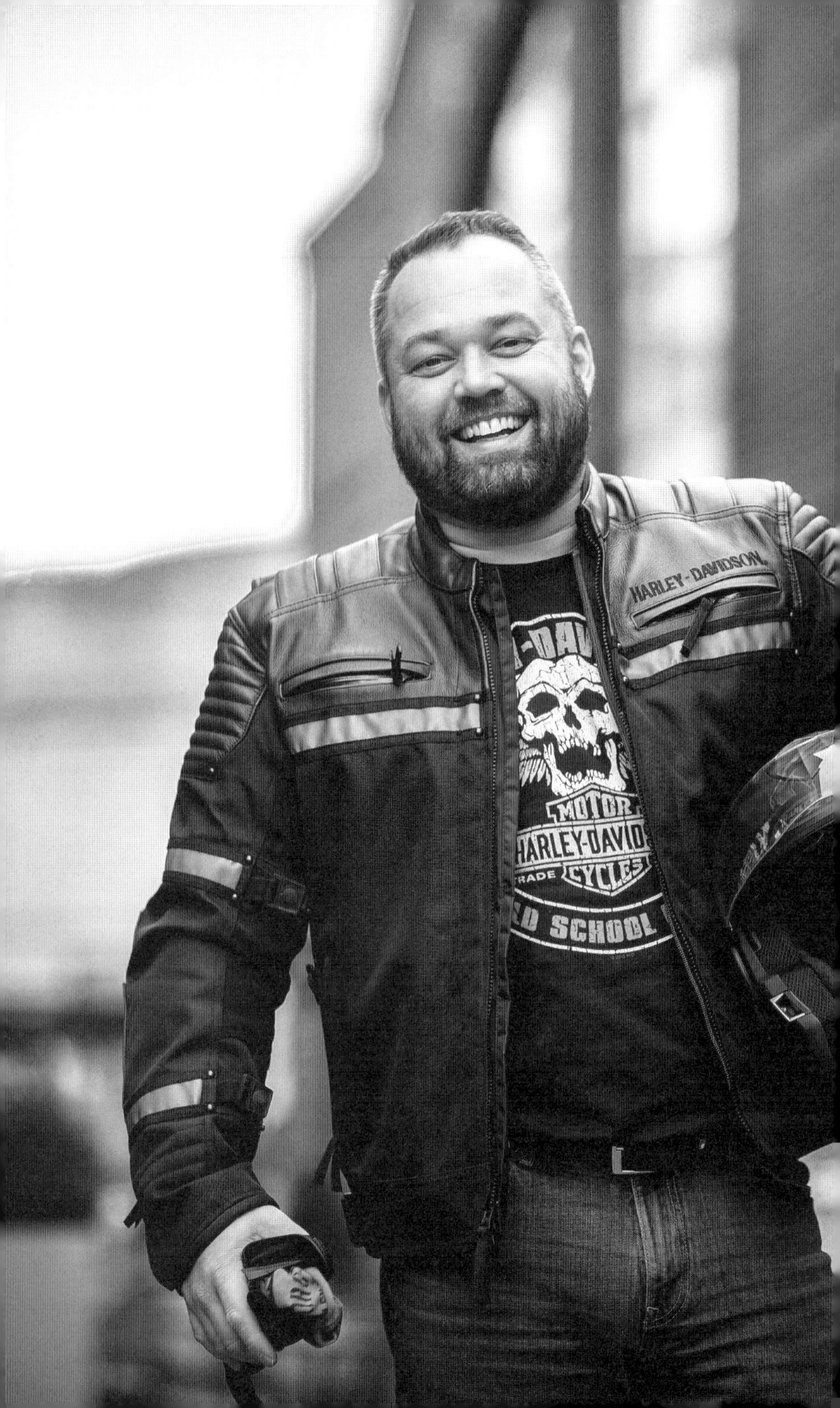
HARLEY-DAVIDSON
MOTOR
TRADE
CYCLES
SCHOOL

Failure is just something to learn from thinks Birmingham entrepreneur John Miller. From a slow start in 1999, his company now makes composites for Formula 1 racing cars and spacecraft.

ENTREPRENEUR 4
THE STUBBORN BIKER
Birmingham

A first look at Birmingham gives the impression of a worn-out city. It has its fair share of old, concrete houses. However this used to be one of the world's industrial laboratories, it was here Watt and Bolton invented the steam engine, Joseph Priestly discovered oxygen and Wedgewood created his famous china. William Murdoch invented the train and the gas-lamp here. Until the 1960s Birmingham was richer than London. Outside the city-centre cars from MG Rover, Jaguar and Range Rover were produced. The Chocolate factory Cadbury had its headquarters here, and the famous Lloyds Bank was founded in Birmingham.

The automotive industry is long gone and the factories are empty. The number of unemployed (10 per cent compared to the national average of 5.1 per cent) echoes the state of the many fatigued buildings welcoming a traveller arriving by train. Yet the city is slowly re-inventing itself through new modern and landmark architecture, and so is the business scene. On the ashes of an era, a new city is being built.

One of the down-to-earth entrepreneurs remaking Birmingham's economy is John Miller. There is a similarity with Gotham City's Bruce Wayne in their shared love of motor vehicles. Yet unlike the Gotham-city benefactor, John Miller neither inherited a fortune nor enjoys staying up all night. He usually tries to catch a good night's sleep, and when he contributes to rebuilding his city he does it from the office or the factory floor during daytime hours. A self-made and growing industrialist with his company "Base Group Limited", he now produces lightweight composites used in Formula 1 racing cars and spacecraft.

His company is a vertically integrated business providing high value technical products and services to aid the manufacture of lightweight composite components. One division is Base Materials, which is an established manufacturer of tooling and pattern materials used by customers in their own production lines.

Complementing their core activities is the production of a range of distributed products, which support advanced composites manufacturing processes. Another division is Base Patterns, which is an engineering business. This provides a fully integrated design and manufacturing facilities.

Base Group serves a range of customers from pipe producers to those building spacecraft. Customers from motorsport accounts for 60% of its revenues. Some of them might spend £20-30,000 per year, while others spend nearly a million pounds sterling.

LEARNING THE TRADE ON THE SHOP FLOOR

His multi-million turnover didn't come from nowhere. He learnt the trick of innovation working with the established players. His first professional experience was with "St Lucas" – one of the major suppliers of state-of-the-art parts for the automotive industry in the 80s and 90s.

16 years old and just out of high school, Miller worked in an R&D department during daytime and studied at night. By 1999, Miller found himself working in the composite materials industry, starting on the production line of a rather large business in Birmingham.

"I ended up in sales" Miller says with a grin. Warm and friendly, it isn't strange he's lifted the revenues of his current company, Base Group Limited, to today's £6.5 million per year.

But returning to the early beginning of his entrepreneurial journey, it started as he saw a growth potential with his current employer. However his ideas quickly met a dead end.

"I suggested for them to spin out a separate entity, which they actually gave me room to do. This would allow me to demonstrate what market potential they were missing out on with that niche product. They accepted it in principle - but wanted to control the execution of it. So I resigned and a couple of months later, I created my first company!" Although his first venture was a hard start, it was a decision John Miller never regretted.

"I was 24 years old. The business idea was to import advance composite materials to the UK market, focusing on motor sport. Only three years into that business we had to close it down, basically due to naivety", explains Miller. The biggest challenge was the creditors meeting, he remembers. The business was liquidated.

Miller entered into an arrangement with a few creditors who were willing to let him try again with the same business idea. Only this time it was with a slimmer number of staff and outsourced warehouse and storage arrangements, which allowed him to focus on sales. The formula proved to work – in just six years turnover grew to £1.6 million.

FIRE

At the time, one of the products alone stood for 50 per cent of revenues. That was a model board which is used to create a pattern or form for a customer's own production line. This has historically been made in wood, and later in aluminium. With the polymer-based substrate he could offer, he provided the market with a better product than what others could supply. The supplier was a US-based firm.

Then disaster hit – the supplier's plant in the US was struck by a catastrophic fire. The factory burned for four whole days. It decimated everything. The result was a plan to establish a joint venture to build a production facility in Europe instead.

"Fast forward to April 2007 – everything went really well. It's 11 AM in the morning and the phone rings. I was at an exhibition in France. It was my partner in the States. The message was: John, I have bad news – I've sold my company to your competitor in the UK so there won't be a Joint Venture with you! The competitor had been the market leader – and we had started to erode their market."

They decided to resolve that issue, explains Miller, by shutting down parts of Base Group's supply chain!

A new disaster had hit. There was only one solution, to set up his own facility, as there were only three/four major suppliers for the products worldwide. Partnering with one of them was not an option. John was able to convince his investors that it would be possible to produce the material, even though they did not know the formula. He basically put on his lab coat and over the next three to four months, with a small team, he got 80-90 per cent of the formula right. That was enough to convince the shareholders. So, by June 2007, they bought a factory. By August, they had set up the plant equipment. By September, they were ready to roll. Or so they thought.

This was just at the beginning of the financial crisis and investors were getting nervous. John could not find the way to get the last 15-20 per cent of the formula right. What they produced at this point, looked like Swiss cheese – the composites were airy and had bubbly holes. They were a small team, and like many SMEs, totally undercapitalized.

"In November 2008, the bank came in, saying: We need to remove your financing arrangement and transfer you to a different scheme. This basically meant they felt the need to babysit us and then to exit with the least amount of damage. So I went along with that." This was hard for the shareholders. They would see a reasonable value disappear and thus started to look for a buyer for the business.

EUREKA MOMENT

However late one evening John Miller had a Eureka moment. He had been at work for 14 hours and was driving home. Then suddenly he knew how to fix it. He drove back to the factory, made a few subtle changes to the formula, and bingo, it worked!

The key was producing the composite materials in a vacuum instead of under normal atmospheric circumstances. Basically his idea was: If there is no air in the making of the product, there cannot be any air in it. The next day, he started manufacturing the new way. Lo and behold – he had solved the problem.

"The question then, was: How quickly could we serve and take on new market shares? The process took us one and a half years. By 2010 we started to sell overseas. First to Italy, which quickly was followed by Switzerland, Germany, Russia, and even New Zealand. After that, we took on the challenge to not only make the substrate, but also to make the prototypes for the customers. Even in the harsh times of 2010 we found some investors. Then – in August 2010 we were able to supply Formula 1 fixtures!"

By now he's really smiling, because in 2012, John was able to buy out his incumbent shareholders. That cost him £300.000, but it gave him the ability to consolidate the group's structure and continue working on developing the brand as well as looking at new product development. Then, by 2015, the board was restructured along with some of the operational staff – and an experienced chairman of the board was brought in.

To John integrity and honesty are essential values. However perhaps an even more important trait is his ability to see the startup phase through to where he is now: his stubbornness. According to himself, his wife has been equally important.

"I don't think my background can account for what I´ve done. My father was a cost accountant and my mum took care of us kids at home. My grandparents also had a working class background, but were very much into engineering. They were all Birmingham-based people. I think the reason I ended up starting new businesses, was that I very much felt restricted. This sense of restriction drove me to it. I thought I could make a difference. I wanted to prove everyone to be wrong, so there was definitely a stubborn element, which is very strong to this day."

THE NEED TO CREATE

His parents divorced when he was about eleven. His mum, being financially restricted, was fortunate to receive social support and a flat and was able to bring up the kids – with the right values, as John puts it. Yet he reckons the years with St Lucas in the R&D department was more formational. Being around those kind of people as a 16-year old was challenging, in the good sense of the word.

There is a sense of pride as the business-biker shares his story. Yet he doesn't seem content for ever. There is more space to grow into. There are more mountains to climb.

"Having the ability to create something. This is the passion that drives me, as well as being responsible for both development and success. There is a great joy in being able to build a good team – and I get a lot of satisfaction seeing growth. Sometimes it is with my own influence – but normally without it", laughs John.

Once the Base Group has completed the consolidation phase it is in now, the focus will again be on growth. John expects that it will come from a number of areas, as the company reaches a wider audience. The aim is to develop new routes to market.

The next phase will be about delivering more innovation. That is new products and new services – first to the existing client base. Then the focus will shift to new sectors. Finally, the aim is to acquire established businesses that complement their activities.

"I will probably not see retirement! There is always more to do! If you always look forward, you take little time to recognize what you've achieved. I always look to the mountain ahead. That mountain now is expanding further into European, Asian and North American markets. There lies our next grand opportunity", says Miller.

I think I see stars in his eyes as he envisions the opportunities.

There have been hard times though. Times where the future did not look as bright as now. How did he deal with those times, facing and going through bankruptcy and laying off colleagues?

THE RIGHT MENTAL ATTITUDE

"Alcohol helps", laughs Miller, admitting he had drowned his sorrows a few times. But on a more serious note:

"Yes, you know, the way you look at the world is important. One has to manage those events. The benefit of failure is ultimately that you persist and then, in the end, you will succeed. If you get it wrong often enough, you will finally get it!"

"That first experience of having to close down a business, lay off three/four employees, and knowing how it impacted their financial stability taught me a lot. I still carry that with me to this day. Now I employ 45 people. That involves families, partners, and mortgages. It's a responsibility I have to those people. When it's just you, it's easy to sometimes move around. When you have accountability to families, there might be no option but to find a solution."

"What were your challenges in scaling up the businesses?"

"For us, scaling up is a constant challenge. As we increase our revenues, we have to find more production capacity. We have to be more efficient. And we have to finance that growth."

He explains that the company have been fortunate. Some of the innovation they have done has been supported by the "UK Trade & Industry".

"They have a vehicle called "Innovate UK" and they have been very supportive of our plans to develop new products. We were not able to find this funding in banks or from private equity firms. The funding they provided for us to explore new product technology has helped us minimize some of the financial impact of that research."

"Tech is on its own the most spoken of and most focused business area in the entrepreneurial world today. How do you believe technology is changing existing businesses, such as manufacturing?"

"For our business, embracing technology means that we may improve our efficiency. Technology works in a tandem with our operational team. Technology allows us to capture more meaningful data to other parts of the business in a more efficient way. It affects the lines of communication, as a business becomes more complex. It's a necessity to be clear about the results we are achieving. So new technology has a place in that – but it will never take over for human workers, I think. I´m not scared of the robots – they won't take over."

"What is possible today, that would not be possible 10 or 15 years ago – in manufacturing?"

"Well for us, the recent developments really help us improve our process control. Which in term improves our product quality. The systems and data we're able to extract allows us to focus on the profitable areas of business, and identify areas that need support. In this respect, technology allows us to improve our diagnostics."

WORK WITHIN THE FRAMEWORK THAT SURROUNDS YOU

"Are there structural issues making your growth more difficult?"

"I didn't start a business to be more tax efficient. I started a business because I believed in what we could do: to provide value to the people we served. Financial incentives are important as the business grows – but not important in the first place to my motivation. You have to work with the boundaries you face!"

"Having a bigger tax break here or in one country or the other is not pivotal to the company being a success or not."

John Miller wears a suit on his company profile, but in real life he prefers jeans and a biker t-shirt in the office. At the end of the day, John really loves motorsport. Now he makes a living for himself and for many others, doing what he loves the most.

FACTS ABOUT JOHN MILLER,

BORN: 1973
CIVIL STATUS: married since 2009. Father of two; Edward (6) and Isabelle (1)
BIRTHPLACE: Birmingham
EDUCATION: High school/college as well as practical experience from the industrial world

What would you do if you were Prime Minister: I would reduce the bureaucracy and make access to finance more achievable for more startups.
What is the best thing about being a UK entrepreneur: It's pretty easy to start something here.

What us the worst thing about being an Entrepreneur in the UK: The possibility that the effort may lead to failure.

THREE GOLDEN TIPS FOR YOUNG ENTREPRENEURS:

1. Firstly: get on and actually start doing something!
2. Learn to fail quickly.
3. Actually learn from the mistakes you do.

APPENDIX 1:
SMART MONEY MAKES NEW BUSINESSES GROW

While Americans are able to build growing companies, Europe is still trailing behind. Luckily, there are signs that a new generation of angel investors is emerging here too.

We saw it in Berlin. The investment scene surrounding the startup boom is maturing, both through the appearance of experienced American investors and the emergence of a new generation of European angel investors. These are young investors in their 30s and 40s who have themselves succeeded as entrepreneurs, and therefore know which types of founder to look for and which businesses have growth potential.

In England, Mark Hart explained that six per cent of startups grow fast and take on numerous employees. In the Netherlands, Professor Jan Sol's job is to contribute to the growth of some of these companies. If Sol meets with spectacular success, the Netherlands will experience a new industrial revolution with a strong rise in employment. By way of example, he points to the industry and university town Eindhoven.

"Eindhoven has a strong foundation of technical skills. We have Philips here, but we don't have experience scaling up companies deriving from the city's existing businesses and universities. If you really want to succeed in high tech, you need to put €100 million behind your effort. You need a hundred full-time employees. A number of these companies easily find ten million to stake, but that's not enough."

Sol highlights a difference between the US and Europe in this area.

"In the US, you have business angels who add both money and knowledge. Until now, we haven't had capital with knowledge willing to scale in this way in Europe. But fortunately, that's changing these days."

At this point that we recall Gonçalo Amorim at the technology accelerator "Building Global Innovators" (BGI). It is a collaborative effort between the University of Lisbon and the Massachusetts Institute of Technology (MIT). BGI's purpose is to build new technology businesses. Newly established companies that join the accelerator are provided solid mentorship, but no money from BGI. This is because in BGI's opinion funds for high-risk startups with growth potential shouldn't come from banks or from taxes, but from the market. That is why companies in the BGI-programme are given vital support to find the right investors.

Examples of this are "USV" and "True Ventures" who, with others, recently invested $29.9 million in "Veniam Works", one of BGI's companies. In addition the seed fund is an important investor in other BGI businesses.

Amorim was frustrated over the general lack of venture capital in Portugal and in Europe, both in terms of available funds and investor knowledge. He feels that this is one of Europe's main problems. In Portugal, it is relatively easy to find money in the first stages of a start-up journey, but then there is almost no growth capital to be found. He says that one can count the number of financing rounds totalling over a million Euros on the fingers of one hand.

In Germany, DIKH finds a similar situation. According to Marc Evers' analysis of entrepreneurship from 2014, 64 per cent of entrepreneurs reported that finding money was a large impediment to growth.

Germany has copied the British SEIS program and called it INVEST. Investors in small and medium-sized businesses under ten years old received a 20 per cent deduction on taxes for investments between €10,000 and €250,000. Starting in 2015, profit on these investments will be exempt from capital gains tax.

At TU Berlin, Jan Kratzer tells us that it can be quite simple finding smaller amounts of money.

"It depends on what field you're working in. It is relatively easy to finance tech companies. But you need

€30 million to start a medical or biotech company. Finding those kinds of sums is challenging."

Max van der Ahé at Betahaus agrees.

"An entrepreneur in Berlin may find a little money, but it's difficult to find a lot of money. Among the Betahaus founders, there are only a few who have found such considerable sums. That means that many companies don't grow. Everyone is talking about it, and it's our biggest problem."

In Portugal Amorim is looking to America to scale up businesses.

"If we're going to build businesses with growth potential, most of the money has to come from the USA. Portugal is a cheap place and a good place to try out new businesses. All the same, companies growing big often move abroad."

"A typical American investor will say, "You know, I love this project, but I hate the Portuguese law, and I don't want to know them either. So, here's what we'll do: we'll leave the engineers in Portugal, but move the main office to the United States. The ecosystem for entrepreneurship in Portugal is good, but I need to have my "baby" somewhere I know it will be safe."

APPENDIX 2:
RESEARCH FOR THE PEOPLE – THAT'S THE THING

Investor money is needed to scale up growing businesses. Universities can invest man-hours. If Europe is once again to create a wealth of jobs, places of learning have to become fresh sources of enterprise.

Access to capital is a problem in Europe. In the Netherlands Professor Jan Sol thinks that universities and research institutes also have to contribute to growing businesses. They can invest knowledge and man-hours, which are just as important as capital.

"TNO can put 20 to 40 full-time equivalents to work on a research project. Everyone has a permanent job and is paid. If we're lucky, after five years, we have a technology that we can sell."

This way of thinking has developed in the Netherlands over the last few years. Sol thinks it's important

This page is sponsored by www.ecpm.info

to establish this strategy among the department heads at universities.

"It's not enough that you have some interested students or one total enthusiast; no one builds a high tech company alone."

It's when new businesses have been started that the road gets bumpy. Often this is when a leadership problem or a lack of sales experience becomes apparent.

"You can often see that the researchers who join new enterprises – or the founders, for that matter – have dollar signs in their eyes. At TNO, we can add technical know-how, but we need another type of person to run the company. And we need a financially capable person to do fundraising, and someone with sales skills. I think the "entrepreneur" or person with the idea should be the director of technology, not the CEO."

Hart and Sol both point to the need to create complementary teams consisting of researchers, sales people and people who know how to scale up.

This is the kind of commercialization that Gonçalo Amorim is working on. His aim is to contribute to creating a market for European technology businesses. In order to infuse the transnational philosophy into its structure and organization, BGI's team is based in Lisbon at ISCTE-IUL, but also in Cambridge (USA) at MIT. To date, BGI has accelerated 117 ventures in six batches, of which 63.8% are still active. It has raised close to €80 million in financing for these in the same period.

Every year approximately 200 companies apply to take part in the program, but BGI only accepts 16 of those.

"We try to give our businesses international mentoring. If you have good mentors then you have every chance to succeed. However, a prerequisite to attract good mentors is that the accelerator has exciting companies in it."

FEW RESULTS FROM R&D

Amorim believes that Europe's problem is that we get little in return for investment in research and development. He believes this is one of the main challenges in Europe when it comes to converting the excellent science and technology developed by Europe's top notch institutions into real innovation that drives the economy and well paid jobs.

"Our philosophy is that universities compete against each other in Portugal, when they should actually be competing with the rest of the world."

Kathrine Myhre at Oslo Medtech shares his opinion. She agrees that it is hard work getting Norwegian investors to get on board, and that they generally have experience from shipping, oil, gas and real estate. As a result they have to be trained to invest in new technology.

"Norway does about ten billion kroner worth of research a year on health. On top of that you have research in IT and other technology development. Universities and research institutions spend little money commercializing the results of their research."

How will investors know if a university has a good businesses model if no one tells them about it? This is why she feels that Norway should stress prioritization of innovation and commercialization in universities' and colleges' budgets.

"Why should scientific production be what is looked at when you're given a position, but the results of your research be inconsequential? We have to stop counting the number of patents and start looking at the number of patents actually being used."

Myhre also wants to alter Norwegian TTOs. They should be less concerned with licensing patents, often to American companies, and more concerned with establishing new companies owning patents.

APPENDIX 3:
THE PROPELLER THAT BUILT NORWAY

Hans Nielsen Hauge (1771 – 1824) and his network forever changed Norway. The Europe of today needs more groups of friends creating jobs for themselves and others.

200 years ago, a farmer's son from Tune in Østfold County created what was to become arguably Norway's first popular movement. In addition to fighting for freedom of religion and expression, he and the growing number of people in his network were driven entrepreneurs, investors and angel investors, who started one enterprise after another all around the country.

During the eight years between 1796 and 1804, and especially during the last five and most effective years of entrepreneurship, Hauge started 30 businesses. If we include the nascent companies he invested in, or was otherwise directly involved in, the number jumps to 150.

In a society that was regularly struck by food shortages and where social mobility was difficult, this had a great impact. As many as 7/8000 were employed at

This page is sponsored by Tomas Heggernes, Bergen

companies owned by Hauge, which means that almost 1% of the working population at the time was employed by him.

On the investment front 1804 was a peak year. Hauge channelled over NOK600 million in today's money into new businesses, more than one per cent of the gross national investment at the time.

Hauge and those that followed him – also known as Haugeans – created political opposition to the king and official rule, they founded schools and social enterprises, volunteer associations and paved the way for the emergence of the welfare state. Considering this, they also paved the way for Norway's democratization.

GRASSROOTS

As a young man, Hauge was ambitious and endeavoured to achieve the same status as the economic and cultural elite. Norway had no aristocracy *per se*, but a rich and powerful class of merchant patricians. The glass ceiling was palpable. Hauge's breakthrough came when he had what he described as a powerful meeting with God in his father's field in Østfold in April 1796.

After this defining moment he realized he was good enough for both God and the elite. It gave him an incredible feeling of freedom, and a yearning to bring others to the Creator. However this would prove to be a challenge. The church monopolized proselytization through the "Conventicle Act", which forbade groups of people gathering to read the Bible without informing the local vicar. When Hauge started preaching and visiting townships and cities all across Norway, household after household became part of the network of friends that contributed to Hauge's free ideas. Although Hauge didn't intend to cause national unrest, his movement helped empower farmers and fishermen with a new responsibility for their own lives.

Commoners were more than ready to receive his message. Politically there had already been tendencies over the preceding years towards opposition to strict royal and government control over the people. Rules like the Conventicle Act and passport requirements for domestic travel had curtailed people's freedom. In the 1790s, Kristian Lofthus led the "Lofthus Uprising", a protest against the onerous taxation. It was brutally crushed and Lofthus himself was jailed and died in custody in 1797.

Hauge was, besides being a preacher and a serial entrepreneur, also a writer. To describe the size of the network that would grow to the Haugean social movement, which has influenced the growth of current-day Norway from the 19th century, the number of books written by Hauge may serve as an example. In a population of around 800,000 people, the total number of his books sold around 200,000 copies. To manage this level of production, he purchased and started a number of printing shops.

This page is sponsored by Helge Haugland, Cape Town

THE NETWORK OF FRIENDS

Three main qualities characterized the movement that arose in Hauge's wake. The first was faith in God and the awakening to a more active Christian life. The reason this was liberating was that the Haugeans took back the right to interpret the Bible on their own, and didn't accept the government clergy's monopoly on religious practice.

The Haugeans' second obvious quality was their building of close ties and fellowship, which contributed to creating new networks of social relations both locally and nationally. Townships in Norway were brought together for the first time, because Haugeans in Hedmark County knew they had likeminded fellows in Stavanger. For the Haugeans inspiration came from Jesus' command to love thy neighbour like thyself. In Sigbjørn Ravnåsens biography of Hauge, we find: "Friends shall endeavour to be frugal and think of their fellows. Such attitudes cannot be developed in egocentric spaces, but in a community where people show humility and let consideration for their fellow man be the key tenet."

The final evident quality among Haugeans was their serial founding. With the success of the many businesses they started, came their desired social mobility and community creation. If an entrepreneur profited from a new enterprise he had started, he wouldn't immediately order new furniture from the continent. Rather, the goal was to establish a private investment fund that other Haugeans could benefit from when they tried starting a business. This also made for social security in a time that lacked the safety net of the welfare state.

Equipping people at grass-roots level in this way helped raise large portions of the populace to the relatively classless society we benefit from today. In addition to this historic effect, we can still see traces of Hauge's work. Hauge's followers started companies such as Møllers Tran, Lilleborg, and Ekornes in Sunnmøre. Other sectors heavily influenced by Haugeans to today include the fishing and shipping industry along the Norwegian coast.

THE NEW HAUGEANISM

Hans Nielsen Hauge became an increasingly large threat to the authorities' quest for control. After a series of short stays in jail, for crimes including breaking the Conventicle Act and traveling and trading without permission, he was imprisoned for ten years in 1804 (excluding a period of freedom during 1809, when the authorities required his expertise to start salt production during the Napoleonic Wars). His case was consistently delayed and Hauge was released, a broken man, in 1814. Nevertheless during his final years he ran several farms in Oslo until his death in 1824.

Together with other currents coursing through the population during the 1800s, the Haugeans and their descendants increasingly took places at the tables where the country's future in various areas would be determined. From being paupers and peasants, they grew to influence the creation of modern-day Norway.

What can we learn from the Haugeans' community building? Firstly, we can see how networks and faith can be a driving force for the will to take chances and take entrepreneurial initiative. Both the social fellowship of their network of friends and their focus on building communities are worth remembering for us as modern entrepreneurs. The power of groups of friends, who built complementary teams, is still important for building businesses with growth potential.

Secondly, their frugal ideals made it possible to use profits not just to increase their own consumption, but rather to reinvest in new businesses. If new jobs are to be created in Europe, ordinary wage earners also have to dare to invest in newly established businesses. First-phase seed money is scarce in Europe, despite enormous surpluses of capital globally.

Thirdly, and perhaps most importantly, it's OK to have ambition and to become good at something. If European startups are ever going to grow beyond small, the will to build something big has to be there.

"Hans Nielsen Hauge is one of the most influential characters in Norwegian history," wrote historian Karsten Alnæs. Hans Nielsen Hauge was likely one of the most important figures in Norway's transformation from a relatively poor agrarian society to a modern, industrial society. Nothing less. The author Arne Garborg even wrote in the novel *Trætte Mænd* [*Tired Men*]: "It wasn't Henrik Wergeland, but Hans Nielsen Hauge, who made 19th century Norway."

The legacy of the Hauge network is still evident – Norwegians are good entrepreneurs. Going forward, we have to show that we can also create those big businesses that provide jobs for the masses.

NICOLAI STRØM-OLSEN is a Norwegian author and editor. He has previously written a biography about the painter Hans Gude and has co-edited several books on topics ranging from human trafficking to business- and regional development. He is co-founder of the art-magazine "KUNSTforum". Nicolai has written the various city-analyses in "Startup Europe".

HERMUND HAALAND is the founder and International Director of the Oslo-based think tank Skaperkraft. He has also founded the website hybel.no, the first Nordic office of meltwaternews.com as well as the innovation conference "Grow" in Western-Norway. He has written the feature interviews in "Startup Europe".

Startup Europe

© Frekk Forlag 2016
© Skaperkraft 2016
www.frekkforlag.no

Photo: Jon Gustavsen
Design: Concorde design

ISBN: 978-82-93097-30-3